Blockbuster Parenting

How Epic Storytelling can Transform your Relationships with Kids & Teens

Kyle Erwin, Ed.D.

Copyright © 2017 Kyle Erwin, Ed.D.

All rights reserved.

ISBN: 978-0-692-94630-5

This book is not intended as a substitute for the medical advice of physicians or mental health professionals. The reader should regularly consult a physician or other licensed clinician in matters relating to his/her health and particularly with respect to any symptoms that may require diagnosis or medical attention.

I have tried to recreate events, locales and conversations from my memories of them. In order to maintain their anonymity, I have changed the names of individuals and places, I have changed identifying characteristics and details.

DEDICATION

To my wife Rachael, the most epic hero I know.

CONTENTS

	Introduction	1
1	Being the Villain	3
2	Being the Mentor	14
3	Being the Anti-Hero	24
4	The MacGuffin	35
5	Life: The Sequel	47
6	Enter the Love Interest	57
7	I Have the Power	67
8	The Big Bad	77
9	Science Fiction	86
10	A Sci Fi Problem	96
11	Foreshadowing	106
12	Heroes of Horror	116
13	Montage Mind	127
14	Deus Ex Leviathan	138
15	It's All Part of the Show!	149
	References	160
	About the Author	169

ACKNOWLEDGMENTS

This work is my personal integration of the best research and ideas I have experienced. Thank you to all the researchers and clinicians who made this book possible.

Thanks to all the teachers and mentors who have instructed me throughout my career.

Special thanks to all the students and parents I have worked with for letting me be a part of their story.

INTRODUCTION

In the story of our lives, we are the hero. We are the protagonist who must make the epic hero's journey to face the dark night of the soul, find the magic elixir, and return transformed to right a tragic wrong by vanquishing the villain. This story structure, most famously outlined by Joseph Campbell (1949), is as old as recorded history. Some have argued that our stories mold the way we think and the path to positive change means changing our story structure (White, 2007). However, the truth is we can't help but make the same story over and over. It's hardwired into our minds. To test this, simply watch an experimental "art house" movie that violates all the rules of story. Most likely you will feel jarred, unfulfilled, or worse, just bored.

From a simplified neurological point of view, the brain hardware creates the mind software. The primary purpose of the system is identifying danger, maintaining survival, and reproduction of the species (Damasio, 2010). The mind is a layered system with basic physical feelings at the bottom, followed by emotions, followed by thoughts, and finally terminating in this thing we call "I, myself" at the top. As an independent "I," my quest is to interact with the world in a way that keeps my family and my-"self" safe and prosperous. To track progress in this endeavor and predict future dangers, the mind creates a "self," an actor to move through a story. The mind devotes significant resources to the autobiographical self that puts all of the pieces together in a whole that makes sense. More specifically, it creates a special kind of sense or pattern that fulfills the primary purpose. It's this pattern that we see play out in movies, books, plays, comics, gossip, politics and even video games.

Learning to accept and harness the power of story can lead to powerful changes. As a professional educator of special needs teenagers and as a psychotherapist, I have found tremendous success in applying this insight. It often begins with the simple question, "What is their story?" Not the story I want to make for them, because that would just be part of my own story. The trick is to see the other person as the hero, it's their story and I'm just playing a part. Sounds simple, but it takes a great deal of practice. I've attended meetings for my students and clients in which the professionals in the room describe the child's problems in terms of their own story preferences: "He was traumatized," "He's not getting enough discipline," "He just wants attention," "He's developmentally delayed." These explanations tend to reveal more about the person making the assertion than the child.

It's the purpose of this book to outline the many ways in which this story technique can be used to aid parents, teachers, and anyone else who works with kids (or people in general). We'll use examples from popular stories to illustrate the points. The example stories were chosen because they exemplify the epic nature of the hero's journey, and because I just like them (hey, it's my story too after all).

Ozymandias realized that taking on the role of the villain was necessary to accomplish his ultimate goal.

As a teacher at a special school for children with "emotional disturbance," I would welcome students into the classroom each morning. In the minds of these teens, every day was a desperate struggle against the horrid adults that wanted to control their lives. I consciously accepted that I am the villain in their story. They would ask me for some special favor upon crossing the classroom threshold, usually small, but the class routine was set. I would simply say "No," and receive the inevitable, "Why." My response, with a wink and smile, "Because I'm cruel and I want to see you suffer."

This dryly humorous response made it clear that I have no problem being the villain. It created a strangely peaceful dynamic in which it was acknowledged that we are adversaries, albeit friendly adversaries as in playing chess. I could say "Good move," he might say, "Wow, you got me." Everything was with a wink and smile. In a more straightforward example, I might say, "I get it that you despise this math assignment, but my job is to do whatever it takes to force you to complete it, so it's okay to be angry and hate me, but the math must be finished."

This technique is nothing new. It has been used throughout the ages, classically by any type of drill sergeant. In the *Harry Potter* series by J.K. Rowling (1997), the character of Professor Snape exemplifies how an adult can consciously choose to be antagonistic to a teen in order to push him in a direction. Specifically, a direction that will never be chosen by the teen, but is in his best interest. In the story of *Harry Potter*, it seems that Snape simply takes pleasure from causing Harry and his friends trouble. So much so that it is assumed he is the ultimate threat of the story, until the reveal that he was working with School Headmaster Dumbledore the entire time. Again, this plot twist is as old as storytelling itself. It's all a variation of the "good cop/bad cop" gambit. When writing or analyzing a work of fiction these processes are so clear and obvious, but something happens to many adults when they attempt to implement the strategy in real life.

Most parents and adults embrace the fact that teens and kids need a villain in their life like Professor Snape who is ultimately on their side and really acting for the greater good. However, many adults also have difficulty stepping out of their own story as the heroic parent or teacher. They take on the mindset of trying to save the poor misguided child. It is easy to fall into this mindset of being the rescuer so one must be on guard to notice it. How can one notice that the hero/rescuer role has arisen? Typically, there is a sign that an adult is heading into trouble with a child and results from both the adult and the child acting from their default heroic position. This necessitates the view that the other person is either the villain to be defeated or the princess to be rescued. The signal of this interaction is the battle itself, the verbal "sword fight" that goes on between them.

Here's basically what it looks like; the adult gives a direction, warning, or even compliment that serves his heroic purpose of molding the child's behaviors or values. The child recognizes this for what it is, an attack on his freedom. The battle is on, and the child wants to win. Many kids learn that it's better to lose the battle and win the war, so they simply submit to the adult and say, "Yes, Sir." However, young children or those with specific types of cognitive impairments might refuse or have a tantrum.

A third type of a child's response is most problematic for adults who can't accept the role of the villain. It's when the child asks that magical question, "Why?" In many cases, this becomes tricky due to the subtle difference between a child that genuinely wants to understand why a direction was given and those who are verbally fencing. I generally like to give the benefit of the doubt by answering the initial "why" query. However, as the adult answers, it's critical to prepare mentally in order to appropriately react to the response given. In some cases, a child or teen might simply ask for the reason, be given a clear answer, and then comply with the direction. Problems arise when it becomes clear that the "why" response was just the opening counterattack.

In sword fighting, there is a basic move called a feint. This is a fake attack designed to look real and provoke a defensive move by the opponent, called a parry. Once the defense is taken, the attacker suddenly switches directions and actually attacks from a different angle. The underlying strategy is provoking a strong defense in order to know how to bypass it. The "why" question is often this feint move. The adult gives a defensive explanation, and now is completely open to counterattack.

The types of verbal attacks open to the child or teen are usually pretty standard, such as: the ever effective, "What if …," the classic "But he got to …," the basic broad attack "You just hate me," or my favorite "If you let me this time, I'll …." The key for handling the situation is noticing that the verbal fencing match exists at all. This is when taking the role of the villain is liberating. To extend the metaphor, the adult figuratively "fights dirty", as all true villains must.

Child: Why?

Adult: Cause it's what I want.

Child: That's not fair.

Adult: You're right, it's not fair. Look, you don't have to like it, you just need to do it. If not, you know the consequences.

The above exchange ends quickly, the child realizes he will lose. An epic example of this type of exchange occurs at the climax of *The Empire Strikes Back* (1980). Luke Skywalker accepts that he has lost to Darth Vader. Luke was faced with a choice; join the Dark Side or be destroyed. Luke lets himself fall into an abyss, accepting that he has lost and makes his choice. Darth Vader looks on thinking, "Blast, that's not what I wanted him to choose, but I know he'll survive and there will be another chance." If the child chooses to not comply and accepts a punitive action, it's not what the adult wants but it's the job of the villain to enact the consequence and move onto other opportunities. Alternatively, the child can surrender and comply by telling themselves, "You may have won this time, but I will beat you in the end." In *The Empire Strikes Back*, Luke looks out into the void of space after recovering from a vicious wound at the end of the film and he thinks, "I may have to run away and hide now, but I will become a Jedi and take my revenge." So the child may begrudgingly follow the adult's direction, but their eyes burn with the hatred of the righteously indignant.

Accepting the role of the villain lets the scenes of life play out to their conclusion, further moving the child along the hero's journey. Trouble often blossoms when an adult is trapped in her own hero's journey having no awareness of the story unfolding and having a need to publicly display her own heroic status.

The comic book hero Batman has faced many different types of villains. The most famous is probably the Joker, who has been written differently over the years but is always chaotic in nature; his motives range from selfishness, to revenge, to sadistic joy in other's suffering. Other heroes face villains of a similar nature. Superman faces off against Darkseid, an alien conqueror bent on total domination of all living creatures. However, many writers claim that the best, most dangerous villains are sympathetic. Villains with goals and values similar to the hero, just slightly twisted. This is often referred to as the "shadow" (Vogler, 1998).

Batman must face many shadow antagonists, most famously, Ras Al Ghul, an immortal super genius who runs an international organization determined to protect the earth from the humans who would destroy it. Sounds heroic, except Ras' solution is to destroy human civilization and thus save Mother Earth. Superman has found his shadow in Lex Luthor, a super inventor whose only goal is to protect Earth from Alien threats, except Lex only trusts himself to judge who is a threat and he's willing to make any sacrifice to expose aliens like Superman as evil invaders. Every heroic character faces their shadow; King Arthur faced Sir Mordred, Sherlock Holmes had Professor Moriarty, and Captain Kirk battled Khan Noonien Singh.

In many cases, the adult and child can engage in this duality, where each sees himself as the hero, producing not just villains but also shadows who believe they are heroes, righteous crusaders who cannot allow themselves to be defeated and must proclaim their virtues at every step. At the heart of conflicts between a shadow and a hero are values. What is worth saving and what must be sacrificed is a value choice. For example, the adult places academic performance as the most critical value, while the child sees individual self-expression as most important. Both are valuable ideals worth fighting for thus creating a conflict. The adult makes clear and logical statements regarding the importance of school for long term success, while the child makes heartfelt pleas for freedom and personal expression. The adult keeps going and becomes more frustrated, aggressive, or enraged that the child does not accept his values. The child makes equally compelling arguments that seem so simple and true he is offended that the adult does not concede. The back and forth builds on itself. Tensions rise. Neither can give up, they must fight the good fight. Until...Boom! Becoming a shadow is the risk of anyone who fights as a "hero." Avoiding this pitfall can be accomplished by playing to the fullest the villainous role the child needs, without expecting any changes in his values (for now).

Being the villain also presents an opportunity to illicit the ideal behavior by engineering a situation in which you appear to be defeated. Many people call this basic idea "reverse psychology." Simply put, say the opposite of what you want. However, this misses the point entirely. To actually change the child's behavior, the adult must take on the villainous role and not try to change a value like in the hero/shadow conflict. The adult is using the child's need to be victorious as a method to change only behaviors and not values. Think of the famous exchange between James Bond and the evil mastermind in the film *Goldfinger* (1964).

> **Bond:** Do you expect me to talk?
>
> **Goldfinger:** No, Mr. Bond, I expect you to die! There's nothing you can talk to me about that I don't already know!

Goldfinger has no interest in convincing Bond that his plans are good. He knows 007 has core values that oppose his perspective. So, Bond is left with a choice; surrender or face the consequences (in this case a slow moving laser). Bond faces the death trap and manages to escape thanks to his ingenuity and fortitude. Heroes of all genres regularly face these death traps and always find a third option, a way of defeating the scenario. This is what children do, and they are extremely good at it. Parents and teachers often set up complex reward/punishment systems only to have the child find a loophole and get the prize without doing any work, or at least not the work the adult wants. This can, however, be used to the adult's advantage.

Child: This math is stupid, I can't do it, go ahead and punish me.

Adult: I know, this new section is very complex. I want you to do yesterday's section over again, then maybe you'll be ready for these new concepts next week. So don't try this new stuff now. You have to wait.

Notice the adult's response did three things. It didn't challenge the value that was being presented by the child, that the math was too hard. The command given by the adult was of equivalent workload since "getting out of work" could be the child's hidden value. Most importantly, it set up that the only way to beat the "death trap" and vanquish the foe was to prove she can complete the new section, the hidden goal of the adult. Children and teens are often fully aware that this manipulation is taking place, that doesn't matter. Their need to win will usually trump their better judgement.

There is one final roadblock to taking the role of the villain and reaping the benefits that come with it. The danger of being halfhearted, of posing as a villain while actually trying to remain the hero. At the conclusion of the film *Raiders of the Lost Ark* (1981), the hero of the film, Indiana Jones is backed into a corner. After all of his heroics, he still finds himself at a loss against overwhelming odds. He is alone against the shadow character, an archeologist named Belloq who controls a vast force of henchmen and has kidnapped Indy's beloved. In a desperate attempt to win, Dr. Jones surprises his adversaries and threatens to destroy the Ark. In essence, Indiana Jones attempts to take on the role of the villain, pretending he has stopped caring about the prize and is willing to sacrifice everything to win. We have seen this many times; the hero attempts to bluff, to portray an image of being hard boiled and willing to stop at nothing to win. Of course, this bluff is easily called. Belloq simply tells Indiana to do it, to destroy the Ark, which of course he cannot. He surrenders, accepting the role of the tragic hero.

Adults often attempt to be the villain, but their heart is not in it. The bluff often works with some children, but not with all. It's also a tactic that degrades over time, since teenagers become experts at calling the "false" villain's bluff. The undeniable sign that parents are in the halfhearted villain role is throwing out ever-increasing strange threats, such as "You'll be grounded for two years if you leave this house." This is an empty threat of a hero trying to fake it. Being the villain means committing. A threat is necessary, a villain simply uses it when appropriate. The teenager says she's going somewhere forbidden, or maybe that she won't be home before curfew. The adult villain glances up from his book and says, "Okay, but you know the consequence, a week of being grounded."

The child leaves sprouting statements about how she doesn't care. The child comes home, and the adult enacts the punishment. "But it's not fair," the teenager laments. The adult responds, "You may be right, but you're still grounded. I hope you remember this next time, but it's your choice."

It sounds simple to fully enact the role of the villain and avoid bluffing, so why is it so difficult in real life? The problem with the above scenario is it involves "grounding." When a child is grounded, so is the adult. He becomes a prison guard. Some teachers like to threaten kids with detention, but then an adult jailer has detention too. There's also the underlying flaw that in the end if a teen decides to leave only physical restraint will stop them, a tactic of last resort that only governmental authorities or authorized professionals should ever attempt. The trick is to have a consequence that is easy to enforce, that takes little work on the part of the adult. Telling the teen that if she leaves the house, she will find her cell phone deactivated for a month has stopped many adolescents from crossing the threshold. This is because they know there's no bluff, a simple phone call, or login to the account and the phone does not work (internet disconnection works well too).

Being the villain to the child's heroic persona can be a great tool, but it can also be difficult to achieve and takes practice. Luckily, there are many other roles to play.

2

BEING THE MENTOR

In the epic story of life, the hero requires a villain, but another type of character is equally critical. It is the mentor, the wise sage, the guide often epitomized in the wise wizard that lives in the tower, the Zen kung fu master who meditates under the waterfall, or the mystical hermit who lives alone in the swamp. Many parents and teachers have difficulty stepping out of their own heroic story to fully embrace being the villain. However, it's somewhat more palatable to embrace the role of the Sage, the all-knowing instructor. Examples of this character abound. In ancient Greek tales, the goddess Athena informed Odysseus on his journey home (Homer & Fitzgerald, 1990). Legends of the middle ages include Merlin who counseled King Arthur in ruling Camelot (Malory & Rhys, 1906). In an epic story of Napoleonic France, Abbé Faria instructed Edmond Dantes to become the Count of Monte Cristo (Dumas, Maquet & Fiorentino, 1934). In modern times, we have Gandalf the Grey Wizard (Tolkien, 1954), Jedi Knight Obi Wan Kenobi (Kurtz & Lucas, 1977), and Professor Albas Dumbledore (Rowling, 1997) who most closely match this archetype. However, the sage can also come in strange and surprising guises, such as the small green alien swamp creature, Yoda (Kurtz & Kershner, 1980).

Many adults seek to take on this role. They take pride in being the mentor to their children, but often this desire to guide the child simply creates more discord. I've worked with many parents and teachers who want nothing more than to show a child the error of his ways, to save him from his own inexperience. What these well-meaning adults don't understand is the basic dynamic of the "mentor" and what is required. Adults who seek to be sages often become usurpers of the child's story, attempting to be the hero by proxy. To avoid this trap, one must clearly understand how to be that wise old wizard (or pointy eared space alien).

In the film *Highlander* (Davis, Panzer & Mulcahy, 1986), the immortal swordsman Connor McCloud was driven from his village when his powers of invulnerability were first discovered. In the film's origin story flashback, the audience is taken to medieval Scotland where Connor is trying to rebuild his life, not knowing exactly what to make of his apparent resurrection. Connor is cut off from his home but has found a new love and seems contented. As our hero basks in his own satisfaction, a strange man literally leaps into Connor's life. It is Ramirez, the mentor and guide of the story who proudly proclaims his intent to train Connor in all aspects of immortal swordsmanship. It's clear what is supposed to happen. Ramirez is dressed in a flamboyant red crushed velvet outfit, he carries an ornate Katana sword, and invokes strange lightning storms from the blue sky. He is clearly integral to this story. To the audience, Ramirez is obviously the mentor. The viewer is excited to see how the training progresses, how he transforms Connor into the hero. However, Connor responds to this mentor as all heroes do; Ramirez is flatly rejected.

Rejection is a necessary part of the hero/mentor relationship. This is evident in story after story. In *Star Wars*, Obi Wan Kenobi implores Luke Skywalker to learn the ways of the force, only to be rejected as Luke races back to the farm to avoid being late for curfew (Kurtz & Lucas, 1977). As the *Sword in the Stone* begins, a young King Arthur rejects Merlin's offer to be his tutor (Disney & Reitherman, 1963). A young James Kirk spurns Captain Pike's offer to join the Starfleet Academy in the rebooted *Star Trek* (Lindelof & Abrams, 2009). The necessity of the mentor rejection is similar to the need for a villain, in that, just as a hero needs a villain to exist, a mentor needs a pupil to exist.

This is confusing for many adults due to the nature of our current education system. In our world, children are forced by law to go to school. Adults assign the label of "student" as the children fulfill their mandate under threat of punishment. A "teacher" is assigned to these children and tasked with instruction. Historically, this system is actually fairly new. It was introduced in the western world in the late 1700s and really only put into firm effect in the 1920s (Gatto, 2001). For most of the history of the world, a student and teacher were created when the master craftsman or scholar took on an apprentice. There was an agreement by both parties. The master would provide valuable instruction in return for labor. It was an equitable arrangement in which the master could delegate the menial chores and the pupil would learn a valuable profession. If either party did not fulfill his obligation, the relationship ended.

For the mentor/hero (master/pupil) relationship to work, both parties must define themselves in the role. They must accept the responsibilities of the role. The master offers training, which inherently comes with a price; the price of being a student and having to submit to the master's authority, the price of taking on laborious duties associated with learning. It's no surprise that a rejection is part of the story as the price of the relationship is quite high.

Many parents and teachers struggle to understand this. They swoop in, and with a grand gesture, offer to be a mentor, to guide the child. The child rejects this offer because they inherently know the terms of the bargain. To accept the offer means playing the submissive student who labors in each assigned task. Adults then become frustrated or just confused. They fail to see that the rejection is part of the story. It's a necessary step. The offer is proposed and the child will not pay the price, initially.

In *Highlander*, after an exchange of insults, Ramirez tosses Connor into the sea. Ramirez knows Connor cannot swim and the hero struggles to avoid drowning. He sinks to the bottom expecting to suffocate, but of course does not because of his superpower. This action clearly communicates to Connor that something is going on that he does not fully understand. Connor realizes he has something to learn. Walking carefully out of the water, sword held high, Connor sneaks up behind Ramirez. The sword swings down, but Ramirez has vanished. A steel blade is at Connor's neck, Ramirez stands ready to cut. With a swish, Connor is disarmed.

> **Ramirez:** Crude and slow clansman, your attack is no better than that of a clumsy child.
> **Connor:** This cannot be, it's the devil's work.
> **Ramirez:** You cannot die, MacLeod, accept it.
> **Conner:** I hate you.
> **Ramirez:** Good, that is a perfect place to start.

In this exchange, Ramirez has made it clear to Connor that not only is there something to learn, but that he is a qualified teacher. Connor says he hates Ramirez because he realizes that now the price of the pupil must be paid. Ramirez takes it in stride, he knows this is the way of things.

If an adult's offer of mentorship is rejected, this is normal. It means the child is not ready to pay the price of the relationship. The adult then has choices. He can attempt to prove his worth as a mentor or wait until the child comes to the realization themselves. Ramirez chose the first strategy, to illustrate the need for a teacher and show off his prowess to be an effective guide. Some adults get this far. After a confrontational exchange, the child will begrudgingly commit to the master/pupil relationship. Interestingly, this is where many adults struggle. They have made their case, the deal is imminent, but now a new price must be paid by the master. The price of being hated. Ramirez gladly accepts this condition. This was understood in apprenticeships throughout recorded history. The pupil despises the master and only forms an openly affectionate relationship once the apprenticeship is complete. Professionals like school teachers, drill sergeants, and corporate leaders, usually have any easier time with this component. For many parents, this is a deal breaker. Adults often struggle to accept a relationship knowing they will be hated. This is due to an underlying confusion and blending of "mentorship" and "friendship."

To avoid this problem and paying the price of being "hated", the prospective mentor can simply wait until the child approaches them. However, this comes with a different kind of difficulty, watching the child suffer. In the *Harry Potter* series, the wise head wizard Dumbledore seems aware of what's going on all the time. He offers profound advice that proves invaluable to the hero Harry. Yet, Dumbledore also seems to stand back and watch Harry and his friends engage in all sorts of incredibly dangerous activities. He watches them suffer, and refrains from offering any mentorship until

Harry approaches him. He waits until Harry has tried his own methods without success and is receptive to advice (Rowling, 1997).

Again, this can be extremely difficult for adults. Parents forever seek to prevent their children from suffering, but to be a mentor, that can be what is required. Although, sometimes the waiting is relatively easy and short. After Luke rejects Obi Wan's offer to be trained as a Jedi Knight and races home, he immediately returns and accepts it after seeing his house destroyed (Kurtz & Lucas, 1977). Similarly, the child might reject the offer of help, try her own way, fail horribly, and then be willing to accept the adult's aid. Of course, sometimes the opposite is true. The child struggles endlessly in vain because she cannot or will not ever willingly pay the price of the master/pupil relationship.

The mentor/hero dynamic has another dimension as well, when the hero initiates the relationship. In classical epic stories, the hero would often be required to make a perilous journey to some far off mountaintop and consult the wisdom of an oracle. Days of agonizing travel through treacherous lands were required, but only those mystics could read the signs of the gods and set the hero on the proper course (Homer & Fitzgerald, 1990). In classical Zen, a prospective student comes to the school and asks the master for instruction. The master would then deny any instruction took place there and claimed no school even existed. The student was expected to refuse to leave. For days, the would-be student was rejected and harassed, until she agreed to all sorts of conditions and was finally granted admittance (Watts, 1957).

In *Star Wars: Empire Strikes Back*, Luke Skywalker travels to the swamp planet of Degobah in order to initiate a master/pupil relationship with an alien creature named Yoda. Luke is rejected as a pupil, he must plead his case and get recommendations from his previous mentor before Yoda reluctantly accepts him (Kurtz & Kershner, 1980). In all these cases, the hero initially believes he is willing to pay the price of the master/pupil relationship. He seeks out the mentor and makes the offer. The rejection of the potential pupil is necessary because often the hero does not actually understand the cost. By making the initial relationship difficult, the hero clearly defines himself in the student role, and whenever the training gets difficult, the mentor can say, "I told you it would be hard."

Children and teens have a tendency to seek out a mentor to get "help." Adults find this request for help encouraging, endearing and flattering. The adult feels special and appreciated for his mentoring abilities. However, without fully understanding the mentor/hero (master/pupil) relationship, the adult can find himself in peril quickly. The problems arise because the child does not really want help. She wants the adult to do the heavy lifting and then let her take credit at the end.

In *Conan the Destroyer,* the epic hero Conan fights a monstrous demigod. He struggles in hand to hand combat and after finally realizing the creature's weak spot, he is able to incapacitate the beast. He then strikes one final time with his sword to ensure the vile thing is dead. Suddenly, Conan's companion and pupil dashes to the carcass, pulls out a dagger, and stabs the monster again. Conan shrugs it off since this attempt to snatch credit is so blunt, it's comical (De Laurentiis, Pressman & Fleischer, 1984). However, this is what children tend to try. They seem desperate for aid, but in the end they have no problem taking credit for the adult's work. I have seen many parents and teachers become exceedingly frustrated when they realize the mentor relationship really does not exist. They are actually being tricked into completing tasks the child simply does not like.

It's critical that when the child approaches the adult for mentorship that the relationship be defined. This can be done by an initial rejection to ensure the child is actually willing to pay the pupil's price. It's accomplished by requiring the student to use her own time to gain access to mentoring. For example, a child wants "help" with a school assignment that should be within their skills to complete. The adult offers to meet with her during the child's "free time", making it clear that the "help" comes with the price of a decrease in preferred activities. In the school setting, I would often offer help at lunch or after school.

Another important aspect of mentoring a child who initiated the relationship is ensuring that all "labor" is done by the child. This includes writing when doing school work or using the tool when completing chores. I sometimes walked in on adults attempting to help a child with school work to see the adult, pencil in hand, hunched over the textbook and paper, talking to themselves. The child is looking at her phone or staring into space.

The final consideration for adults taking on a role of the mentor and sage is the need to leave the story. In the epic story of life, the hero is trained and set off on her quest. The mentor follows and guides her, but at a critical point the mentor leaves the story (for a while). In *Highlander*, Ramirez trains Connor in the art of swordsmanship to the point Connor is able to best him in a duel. Ramirez explains the rules of being an immortal swordsman and the competition that drives them forward. With the primary goals of bestowing the skill of sword fighting and the knowledge of the quest complete, Ramirez leaves the story (by getting decapitated by the villain). The same is true for Obi Wan Kenobi, who gives up in the middle of the lightsaber duel with Darth Vader and appears to be eviscerated. Gandalf the Grey Wizard sacrifices himself to stop the monstrous Balrog. Merlin is imprisoned in the crystal cave. Examples abound. The mentor must leave the story for the hero to face the "dark night of the soul," the low point that each hero must overcome alone. Many adults struggle with this exit. The adult fears the child will not succeed and parents often crave guaranteed success. However, for the child to truly be the hero, they must succeed on their own, and sometimes heroes fail. Throughout the epic story, the hero experiences failure, some great, some small. This is necessary to move the story forward, to learn and grow.

Letting the child fail can be tremendously difficult, but again it is required. Of course, the mentor returns if absolutely needed. Throughout the story of *Highlander*, Connor recalls the lessons he has learned from Ramirez and how he's applied them over the centuries to become the winner of the "prize." In a more acute situation, Luke Skywalker is flying in to destroy the Death Star and save the day, but he's not applying the lessons he's learned, he needs a small push. He hears the voice of Obi Wan, "Use the force" and Luke knows what to do. Gandalf returns as the White Wizard charging into battle. The mentors return when they are absolutely necessary and in proportion to that need. Connor just needed to remember the wisdom he was taught, Luke needed a small verbal prompt, and Frodo needed a full blown physical intervention with a sword-carrying Gandalf riding in on a white horse.

In our world, the adult mentor decides to back away, sometimes even creating situations where the child must finally go out alone. Going to school for the first time, attending "sleep away" summer camp, and leaving for college are necessary situations to force children to confront challenges alone. These steps towards independence carry danger and risk, but the adult mentors must let the hero try, fail, and try again. If she needs help, give it in the mentor fashion; a small reminder of past lessons to boost confidence, a short verbal prompt that puts them in the right direction, or if necessary, riding to the rescue. Many adults struggle to not jump immediately to the most intrusive method. They're primed and ready to leap on the white steed and charge in! This may be required, but it must be a last resort and once the child can stand on her own, the mentor again leaves the story. There is a strong compulsion for most adults to stay in their own heroic mentality, and save their child from failure. This is not a terrible thing, but it keeps the child from moving forward in her own story. It keeps her from growing. Being the mentor is a choice that can be greatly beneficial to children, but it's most effective when fully understood. Sometimes it may not be the best role to take, and fortunately there are other approaches.

3

BEING THE ANTI-HERO

A group of teenage boys walks into the classroom. One after another, they trod slowly, all wearing black clothes. Some wear "heavy metal" t-shirts with elaborate artwork depicting skulls, bones, and demons of all kinds. Others wear plain black hoodies, their faces hidden in the shadows with long bangs hiding the eyes. Some wear dark shirts with monograms of strange symbols representing "dark" pop culture references. A few go all out, with symbols of "anarchy" and "Satanism" on proud display. Clothes depicting characters from video games, comic books, movies and television are also widespread. These characters carry swords, knives and guns of all kinds. They include characters like Spawn (a vengeful spirit returned from hell), Deadpool (a rogue assassin who is invincible), and the Punisher (a psychotic vigilante who murders criminals). The bands, the characters, and the symbology change over the years as new teenagers come and go from the class, but one thing is constant; these teens are proclaiming the role of the "anti-hero."

The idea of the "anti-hero" is as old as storytelling, with the term originating in the 1700s. The anti-hero is the center of the story like any protagonist, but unlike the traditional hero who fights to vanquish evil, anti-heroes seem to fight only for themselves. It is important to understand that this apparent selfishness is only skin deep. In the end, the anti-hero always does the right thing, but not necessarily for the right reasons. They may achieve their goals through morally questionable methods, but they also maintain a strict code of honor. This code traditionally runs askew of the dominant moral paradigm. For example, the Punisher murders criminals constantly but refuses to shoot police.

One day in my class, a boy with an extreme history of abuse and violent outbursts (dressed all in black) decided he would sit in a different chair. Each seat was assigned, so this was an act of "rebellion." When prompted to return to his designated spot, the boy leapt to his feet and declared in a storm of profanity that he would not obey my "rules." To add gravity to this pronouncement, he kicked the small trash can in the front of the room, bits of paper and refuse flew across the floor. My response was designed to exploit his "anti-hero" persona. In a calm manner, I explained how I accepted his decision and knew he was willing to face the consequences of his actions due to his strong principles. However, I also noted that it seemed unjust to me that I should have to clean up the trash because he disagreed with a school policy. I then turned to the class and resumed my lesson, the boy remained standing in front of the room, seething and ready for a fight. A few minutes passed. The boy sat down in the wrong chair to maintain his rebellion. More time passed, the lesson continued, the trashed remained strewn across the carpet. Without warning, the boy silently sprang to his feet, quickly picked up all the trash, replaced the can in its rightful position, and sat back down. In the next class, he sat in his assigned seat. I didn't make any further comment about it and he never went against a classroom rule again (at least in my class).

What just happened? If he wasn't punished or reprimanded for his actions, why did his future behavior change in my class? The boy was caught in the grip of an anti-hero fit against the "man." He might have been Dirty Harry telling off the Mayor, or Conan punching out the palace guard (Siegel, 1971; De Laurentiis, Pressman & Fleischer, 1984). He wanted a confrontation in which he was the crusader against the banal and corrupt establishment. I did not give him that. Instead, I shifted the conflict away from the rebellion issue, (not sitting in the assigned space) and made the focal point the trash can. But, even though it was a rule violation, I only spoke of the unjustness of me having to pick up trash due to his rebellion. He picked up the trash because the anti-hero does what is right in the end, but will never admit it. It was critical that I didn't acknowledge his act, not even with a "thanks."

Traditionally, if asked, anti-heroes will disavow any intention of helping other people without personal gain, but when the chaos ensues, they act to save the day regardless of pay. Alternatively, the anti-hero maintains a myopic obsession with a particular goal and will claim to sacrifice others to reach that goal, but again it's just a bluff.

There is a special attraction to the anti-hero for many people, especially teenagers. This phenomenon is often confounding to adults and parents, but by understanding the role of the anti-hero, adults can better work with kids and teens. Sometimes, even taking on the role can be of tremendous benefit. In many ways, a teen's perspective is paradoxical, seeing the world in black and white terms, but not with simple right vs wrong dichotomies. Teenagers have a unique perspective in that they are learning the "society game," all the rules that adults take for granted. Often adults believe these rules will be absorbed through osmosis, with no need for direct instruction. On the occasions when adults do spell out the rule, the rules don't make sense.

Adult: Stay in your assigned seat.

Child: Why?

Adult: Because I'm the teacher and you must respect my authority.

The actual reason for rules and procedures might be extremely justified but generally are simply centered on a particular value. Children sit in assigned seats because they're less likely to interact with kids they don't know. The goal is a quiet classroom where kids are easily directed towards the teacher. Of course this comes with a price, as the children themselves feel tremendous anxiety being surrounded by strangers and can seek desperately to alleviate this sense of isolation. An adult might explain the actual reason, and children may understand it, but in the end they will argue in some fashion for the option that matches their emotional value; teens want interactions with their peers, adults want quiet.

Anti-heroes fight for simplified values, "justice," "vengeance," "equity." The real world is profoundly complex where randomness and the rule of unintended consequences dominate. However, to the teen's concrete way of thinking, centering on these simplified anti-hero types of values as guidelines feels more natural. Psychology has thoroughly documented the process of heuristics in the human mind. These are "rules of thumb" that form the basis of all decisions, biases, and stereotypes. They are hardwired in the human mind and lead to some interesting phenomenon. More importantly, they operate below the radar of conscious thought and lead to decisions that seem completely justified, but in reality are based on subjective emotional values (Ariely, 2010; Kahneman, 2015). An anti-hero acts from this place of simplified emotional values. To work effectively with teen anti-heroes, the values they fight for must be identified and exploited.

For example, many teenagers get hung up on "equity" since they have so many limitations and are surrounded by adults who don't seem to be anymore entitled to drive, drink, and gamble than they are. Yet, these activities are barred to them based solely on their age, something completely outside their control. This feels inherently unjust. In the schools, some argue that adults should follow the same rules as the children to not trigger the anti-hero reaction to inequality. However, this is a disservice to teens and a missed opportunity. In my class, a rule existed that no food or drink was allowed in the main areas where class was conducted. However, I flagrantly sipped from a mug of coffee throughout lessons. Inevitably, this was deemed "unfair" by a student. I would agree that it was "unequal" and that I was enjoying a privilege he did not have. I explained that to be "unfair," then each student must graduate high school, earn a bachelor's degree from an accredited university, complete a student teacher internship, get credentialed by the state as a teacher, obtain a teaching position in the school and then be denied the right to drink coffee in the classroom. I noted that any student who went through the same steps as I did would most likely not be denied the privilege.

Many parents have used this same gambit, but the trick is in the sincerity of the delivery. A parent's flippant statement of "When you pay the bills, you can do you what you want" feels like a cop-out. If the child believes that his moral objection has been addressed in a serious and thoughtful manner at a level of value the conflicts can be resolved. I outlined my struggles to become a teacher in terms of actionable steps that they too can take. I invite them to begin their journey, for example, by starting classes at community college to expedite their degree. A parent's "When you pay the bills" is often met with a retort of, "Fine, I'll get a job and move out." This of course is unlikely, but nothing has changed to end the conflict. The underlying value has not been addressed and the verbal fencing match continues. The anti-hero remains in full righteous indignation mode, just as when Detective "Dirty" Harry Callahan throws his badge on the desk and threatens to quit the police or when Wolverine is told to wait for the rest of the X-men just before charging off solo to stop the villain (Siegel, 1971; Donner, Winter & Singer, 2000).

Another trait of anti-heroes is that they don't talk about things, they act. The anti-hero doesn't discuss, debate, or plan, they jump into the fray while everyone else is still contemplating. Again, this is a function of an emotionally driven behavior based on simplified moralistic values. For example, in *Conan the Destroyer*, the anti-hero, played by Arnold Schwarzenegger, is confronted by a group of religious zealots. In their fantasy realm, these people worshiped an ancient deity whose magic item they protect. Conan has stolen this item for a princess who is supposedly chosen to wield it. The wizard who leads the zealots tries to explain their position; they can't let the item be taken, however they do accept the princess as the chosen one. There is room for negotiation in the situation, and another protagonist might broker a deal since their goals are not completely out of alignment. Conan works for a queen who is a worshiper of their deity as well. However, Conan, in true anti-hero fashion, bellows, "Enough talk!" and throws his dagger into the gut of the wizard. Chaos ensues. Conan is impatiently operating under a simple moral imperative; get the princess and the magic item back to the queen to collect the reward and he is unwilling to be sophisticated in achieving this goal. Instead, he acts with blunt and rash actions to meet his objective in the most direct and quickest way possible (De Laurentiis, Pressman & Fleischer, 1984).

Teenagers in the anti-hero mindset are similarly quick to action. If they get insulted by another student at school, they might punch him in the face. If they're going to fail a test, they might cheat. If they're forbidden from seeing that special girl/boy, then they sneak out. These behaviors seem shortsighted and selfish and appear to be outgrowths of corrupt morals. However, as discussed in the previous chapters, children and teens see themselves as heroes, but when there is an anti-hero orientation the rules change slightly. The morals are usually anti-establishment and self-justifying. When they are insulted in school, the value "Bullies should be taught a lesson in the only language they understand" leads to a punch in the face. If a student is unprepared for a test, a value of "Stuff in school doesn't matter in the real world, it's just a way to control me" results in cheating. If they're grounded and can't see a girl/boyfriend, then the value of "True love is all that matters" equates to sneaking out of the house.

To handle this reality, parents and adults must first recognize the anti-hero persona. This must come with purposeful acceptance that no amount of explanation about long term consequences will matter. In this situation, a complicated set of rationale will not trump simple emotional values. However, equally simplified alternative values can be offered instead. For example, "Resorting to violence means you lost," "Cheating is the coward's way out," "If she really loves you, she'll wait." These are the types of heuristics that an anti-hero lives by. Of course, the other part of dealing with children anti-heroes is to realize that there's most likely nothing you can do to change their mindset. Similar to taking on the role of the villain, a parent can become the "by-the-book police captain," or the "out of touch superior officer." Dirty Harry argued with his captain in almost every scene they shared, but in the end, Harry obeyed the orders because he was given basic short-term strong arm threats such as, "You don't take a partner, you don't have a badge" (Siegel, 1971).

Now a few words about Batman. Many people would categorize the Dark Knight as an anti-hero. I would argue this is incorrect. Yes,

Batman lives by his own moral code and is willing to break the law to achieve his goals. However, Batman is dedicated to a long-term mission of justice, not revenge. The idea of real justice is complex with many facets. A champion of justice must consider unintended consequences and make complex moral judgements using a predefined framework such as utilitarianism. Batman is a character who has chosen to pursue a never-ending mission to bring justice to anonymous strangers. He developed a complex framework for his crusade which, in most incarnations, includes a moratorium on lethal attacks. He trained for years with great masters in many disciplines (Weldon, 2017). He painstakingly strategizes, examining situations from every angle. This is exemplified in Mark Waid's (2001) *Justice League* story "Tower of Babel" where Batman's elaborate fail safe plans are used to incapacitate each member of the Justice League, including Superman.

If teens were more like Batman, most parents would be elated. Some classify Batman as an anti-hero mostly due to the version created by Frank Miller (2015) in *The Dark Knight Returns*. That version of Batman was hyper focused on brutalizing his opponents to reach his short-term objective. His actions were part of a psychological need to "fight." His rules were the simple heuristics of the anti-hero, for example, "Guns are the weapons of cowards." There have been many versions of Batman, but in general, the character is a study in the difference between strategic long term thinking and impulsive actions based on simplified value driven rules of thumb.

The glorification of "impulsiveness" is not the only attractive quality for teens. They often relate to the anti-hero due to their focus on winning through brute strength and sheer willpower. Teens often feel powerless, but many are able to find solace in particular activities, such as good grades in school, proficiency in sports, or creative pursuits. Some handle the feelings of powerlessness by standard techniques like journaling or just complaining to their friends. Unfortunately, some adolescents even turn to destructive activities like substance abuse, eating disorders, and criminal conduct. All of these behaviors are means of feeling in control.

Teens without adequate means of finding a feeling of control may resort to the primary method of brute force. In my experience, this anti-hero belief in the power of rage is quite pervasive among teenage boys. The anti-heroes of movies, TV, and video games will win the day through a sudden burst of aggression, usually accompanied by an intensive yell or shout. The techniques of shouting to enhance physical endurance is obvious to any sportsman such as when tennis players grunt, football players growl, and martial artists "Kiai."

However, teens who envision themselves as the anti-hero overcoming anything through "rage" may exhibit overconfidence and choices that are problematic. I have witnessed many teen boys hurt themselves when hitting a wall or other object thinking that their "rage" will give them the strength to overcome materials like bricks. One boy broke his hand trying to smash a plate glass window. This sounds strange, but that is the nature of the anti-hero mindset, which works in fiction, but not often in reality.

In the sci-fi adventure *Total Recall* (Feitshans, Shusett & Verhoeven, 1990), Arnold Schwarzenegger's character has been captured and all seems lost. But filled with rage he rips out steel restraints to escape and win the day! Watching the film, this seems possible, it makes emotional sense, but reality is far different. As part of the "restraint team," I've had the unfortunate duty to physically restrain teens who are in imminent danger of harming themselves or others. In these situations, we are trained in specific techniques to ensure that the chance of injuries are as minimized as possible. The techniques take advantage of leverage so that no matter how much force is exerted by the one being restrained, they are not able to move, but little force is exerted by the restraint team, thus further reducing risk of injury. The length of these encounters varied greatly. The teen was released when it was clear he was no longer in crisis and safe. I was amazed at the number of instances where these encounters could last up to an hour, even more. In these cases, the child or teen was convinced that with enough rage they could break free and hurt themselves or attack their intended target. The restraint team leader was specifically trained in speaking to teens in crisis so they understood that calming down was the way to end the situation. Yet, the struggle always lasted longer than it should.

Understanding that some teens believe rage gives them the power to win can help adults in conflict with teens. When they make threats about breaking down doors or beating up others, it's no bluff, they often genuinely believe in their strength. Adults can help de-escalate the situation by avoiding a direct challenge to the teens' boasts and instead focusing on the underlying emotional need to feel in control. Validating the teens' perspective to help them calm and then aiding in using other strategies can be effective. Again, this requires adults to maintain their emotional center in the face of highly escalated situations and irrational individuals. However, irrational behaviors are not the same as unpredictable behaviors. Anti-heroes believe in their power to control through force of will; challenging that belief with logical debate is worthless, yet this is often a go-to method for adults. When a teen is acting in an anti-hero role, validating the emotional pain that is taking place is the best method to de-escalate the situation, logical discourse comes later.

There is one aspect of the anti-hero that parents may consider taking on themselves. The fact that adults like to talk too much to kids is almost cliché, yet it happens all the time. If the teen's default mode is that of the anti-hero, then talk is cheap. Only actions matter. The stronger and more decisive the action, the more "bad ass" it is to teens. Parents who talk about morality and ethics but never demonstrate through actions will most likely not effect a teen. Taking time to recognize opportunities of being the anti-hero can be incredibly powerful. These opportunities can be big or small, often or rare. They can be big like taking a day every month to volunteer in the community or small like simply not laughing at a racist joke. Any chance to channel the inner Dirty Harry, to exude confidence in an ethical decision by simply taking actions and talking as little as possible. This is the way to impress teenagers.

4

THE MACGUFFIN

The fedora wearing hero, Indiana Jones, creeps carefully through the ancient labyrinth avoiding diabolical traps, treacherous backstabbing guides, and unrelenting competitors (Marshall & Spielberg, 1981). He does this because he is on a quest, a mighty quest, a glorious quest, a quest for the ultimate prize, the most valuable of all possessions. In movies, the hero is seeking something, a goal. This goal might be a person/relationship, it might be a job, it might be to reach a certain location, but most often it's to obtain an object. All these goals are known as the "MacGuffin." This term was made popular by Alfred Hitchcock in his discourse on filmmaking. Examples of the MacGuffin are easy to find in movies: The Maltese Falcon statuette, the Ark of the Covenant, a small droid, or simply a nondescript silver briefcase (McKee, 1997).

What makes a MacGuffin interesting is the fact that it must be in the story. If not, the film feels strange or incomplete. Many filmmakers and storytellers will say their story is about something abstract such as "deconstructing middle class values in the light of new globalist interest" but these esoteric statements are about the theme, not the story. A story is about a character trying to get something, to do something, to go somewhere. Both levels need to exist for a story to feel satisfying, including the obvious quest for the thing as well as the underlying quest of the character for self-actualization. The two levels might simply lay on top of each, such as in *Raiders of the Lost Ark*. Indiana Jones is trying to get the Ark of the Covenant and has many adventures in this quest to possess an object. Underneath the external story, it's about Indiana searching for faith and being able to "let go." This is seen in the climax of the film when he decides to close his eyes when the Ark is opened. He had been transformed through his adventure and accepts that supernatural powers exist. Closing his eyes is also symbolic in that he accepts "not knowing" that some things are best unseen, which is opposite from his attitude at the beginning of the movie (Marshall & Spielberg, 1981).

The MacGuffin might also be more complex such as in *The Matrix* where the hero Neo is searching for "The One" who is going to destroy the machine empire. The twist is of course that he himself might be "The One", so simply put, Neo is on a quest to find "The One" in himself. This seems extremely abstract but it's just another flavor of a character trying to reach a tangible goal. In this version, the hero's inner journey of self-acceptance is more obvious and on the front lines, but without the measurable goal of "I am the One," the movie does not work (Silver, Wachowski & Wachowski, 1999).

The MacGuffin exists in stories because people can't help but establish goals. These goals might be long ranging, such as a child saying they want to be a doctor, or they may be short like, "I want a hamburger for dinner." Goals define a person's story. Many goals exist at the same time and are often at paradoxical odds with each other. When working with teens, I've found tremendous advantage in discovering and accepting the current MacGuffin in their story. Also, rarely has the focus of their quest been the same as my focus. My quest may be for students to increase their reading scores, while their goal is to level up in a video game. Many adults attempt to persuade teens to give up on their quest and change their goals to a MacGuffin that aligns with the adult's desire for them. Darth Vader suggests that Luke give up on becoming a Jedi and join him in ruling the universe (Kurtz, & Kershner, 1980). The evil archaeologist Belloq tries to convince Indiana Jones to join him with the Nazis and find the Ark together (Marshall & Spielberg, 1981). Watching these exchanges, we the audience know the hero can't give in, they must stay the course and fight toward the goal that the movie is all about. Again, adults who gets stuck in their own story will not be able to effect changes with teens. For teens, pursuing the goal is all that matters. Parents will then often attempt to bribe teens with promises of special privileges or threaten them with tortuous punishments. Darth Vader tells Luke he must join the Dark Side or be destroyed, Belloq tells Indy that he'll be killed if he continues to interfere. Again, a hero does not concede to temptation or threats of adversity.

To work with teens' MacGuffins adults must create the challenges that heroes face on the way to their goal. In my classroom, getting the teens to complete assignments was a continual issue so I worked it into their MacGuffin. They all had specific personal goals that were overwhelming and immediate. Indeed, because of their particular emotional and neurological disorders, the drive to obtain his or her current biggest MacGuffin was inescapable. Most teens have goals that would fit into the romantic comedy genre in which goals are pursued slowly as the characters go to work and complete daily chores. However, my students and many other teens feel like they live in a blockbuster action movie where every second not spent in pursuit of the goal is a ridiculous waste of time. Imagine if Indy decided to do some mundane chores like laundry before setting off to stop the Nazis. No, his shirt grows more dirty and torn as the adventure unfolds. However, there are scenes where Indy must change his clothes and get cleaned up. When he needs to infiltrate the Nazi base, he steals a uniform and is directed by another Nazi officer to comb his hair. Indy complies just long enough to turn the tables and then continues towards his goals. In "The Last Crusade," Indiana has several costume changes to infiltrate Nazi strongholds complete with fake accents to match the costume. He is willing to take these actions because they are a direct and necessary step toward reaching his goals, getting the Ark or rescuing his father. Applying this concept helps adults incorporate limits and rules into a teen's world (Marshall & Spielberg, 1981; Watts & Spielberg, 1989).

For my students, completing the assignments to my specifications was the trial to advance towards the MacGuffin. The teens would push through the assigned task with speed and fervor, turn it in, and go back to their personal pursuits, the same as Indy placating the Nazi guard for only those few necessary seconds. It was then my job to add another obstacle to the teens' goals when their completed assignments did not meet my specifications and corrections were needed. Often, with a groan and fierce expression, one of the students would snatch back the paper to make the corrections. Sometimes this exchange occurred many times over and over. Finally, when the quality would be satisfactory, the student had earned the right to return to his or her personal mission. I considered this a good transaction because we both came away winners. This only happened because I stayed in their story. I was the obstacle, a trial in the second act that each hero must overcome to keep pursuing his MacGuffin.

Many adults have problems with this approach. They strain and lament that teens do not just change their goals and accept the adult's MacGuffin as their own. This distress is often the result of comparing the MacGuffins of each person and believing that one is more worthy than another. For decades, filmmakers didn't think the MacGuffin's details really mattered. One was just as good as another. It was believed that the audience doesn't need to know or care about the object in question, as long as the character does. For example, suppose the whole world is at stake because of an object about the size of a pen. This object is lost and must be retaken before the bad guys get it and use it for nefarious purposes. In the spy thriller *Ronin*, the MacGuffin is reduced to a silver briefcase that government agents of all kinds will kill and spend millions to obtain. We the audience never find out what was in the briefcase, but it doesn't matter, the movie still works (Mancuso & Frankenheimer, 1998). Interestingly, George Lucas and Steven Spielberg famously went against this thinking by proclaiming that the substance of the MacGuffin matters. The droid R2D2 in *Star Wars* is a MacGuffin that is fun to watch with just enough backstory to be intriguing without being boring (Kurtz & Lucas, 1977). In *Raiders of Lost Ark*, the Ark of the Covenant tweaks all kinds of emotions by being a holy object in numerous religions (Marshall & Spielberg, 1981). While I acknowledge that interesting MacGuffins make better movies, I believe that when working with teens, it's best to take the view of Hitchcock and Ronin. Teens' objectives are not ours, and that's okay. Goals change constantly, they're layered and in a few short years it's possible that adult and teen MacGuffins will align. For now, just recognize that the MacGuffin is there and you don't understand it, it's a silver briefcase with something in it that teens will do anything to get. It can also help to keep in mind that what is a simple briefcase for us is actually the Ark of the Covenant to teens. We adults don't need to share this belief, just understand it.

Normally the MacGuffin is the big overarching goal that takes precedence over all others. However, what if there are two goals of equal importance? What if there are two MacGuffins? This of course is reality for all people. We have potentially hundreds of goals in play all the time. Our current MacGuffin is what's been prioritized as most important. This is not a conscious choice. We manage our many goals by subconsciously prioritizing them into levels. A top number one goal is followed by a number two goal, which is of near equal importance, and an endless row of lesser quests are stacked behind them. These are the quests we plan to take up one day, but they can wait. Of course there is emotional distress that comes from not obtaining our current top goal. That distress is the fuel for the quest and what drives us forward. A different kind of emotional distress occurs when two goals are positioned at the same mental level, when two MacGuffins are equally important to our subconscious mind. Many times we can deal with this distress by making a difficult conscious choice to prioritize the goals, to force a number one and number two. The choice is made easier when both goals can eventually be pursued, but what if these goals are mutually exclusive or paradoxical in nature (Carey, 2006)?

In *Action Comics* #719 (Michelinie, 1996), Superman's significant other Lois Lane is delivered a strange doll. She is immediately worried and for good reason, because it's from the maniacal Batman villain, the Joker. It seems Lois ran afoul of the Joker by publishing a story that foiled one of his plans. Unfortunately for Lois, the Joker designed the doll to transfer a strange poison into her bloodstream during the brief moment that she held the doll. Joker's poisonous concoction would kill Lois in exactly two hours! With Lois in the hospital, Batman and Superman both confront the Joker who is easily located in Arkham Asylum. Superman demands an antidote, which the Joker surprisingly delivers without delay. There is a catch of course. The vial he produced was only one part. The Joker explains that to make the actual antidote, Superman must inject Joker with the serum which will kill him immediately as Joker's blood is transformed into the antidote that will save Lois' life. Superman does not kill so he is faced with goals/priorities of equal level in that he must save Lois, but also he must never kill. Superman, the most powerful individual on the planet is crippled with intense emotional pain. He is rendered powerless. It takes Batman's cold moralism to save the day as he helps Superman prioritize conflicting values. He reminds Superman that he cannot save everyone, he is not all powerful. This is not a possible choice. However, he can make the choice to never kill, this is within his power. Superman painfully accepts this new prioritizing. He leaves to be with Lois. Of course, Lois does not die. She suddenly recovers without any intervention. Superman is confused and Batman explains that the serum Joker offered would have certainly killed the "Clown Prince of Crime," but would have done nothing to aid Lois. Batman deduces that the plan was to drive Superman into madness by tricking him into taking a life when it wasn't actually necessary. A stunned Superman is reassured by Batman that Joker's plan was insane, but after all, that's the Joker. Of course, most of us have witnessed similarly self-defeating behavior in many children and teens.

Adults often have long and arduous talks with teens about morals and ethical choices. This is good. Teens and children benefit greatly from honest discussions about complex problems. Unfortunately, many of these talks are not discussions, but persuasive speeches by adults trying desperately to rearrange the cognitive priorities in children. Parents employ rationale logic chains and "trap" questions, where children are asked questions with obvious answers that support the adult's position. The truth is often that teens already accept the value that is being presented. They want to succeed in school, stay safe, and make their parents proud. However, they usually have equal cognitive beliefs about being liked by peers, getting a date with that special guy/girl, or simply being right. Teens have tremendous anxiety and guilt about the inevitable instance where goals clash. When that happens they can become paralyzed with emotional distress just as Superman did. The adult's job is not to convince teens that a certain goal is worthwhile, or even that one is more important than the other. The adult acts as Batman did and brings attention to the mental processes going on.

When goals clash, parents can point out that pursuing both goals has tremendous merit but the teens must work out which goal has priority. An adult can offer guidance but teens must do the work. Asking questions is a great tool in this process as long as the questions are posed with honest acceptance of the importance and power of both goals that seem to be clashing. Being with that certain boy/girl is the "Ark of the Covenant," the "Death Star Plans," or "the One" while goals that adults favor, like "getting into college," are more akin to the nondescript silver briefcase of Ronin. They know it's important, but they only know because adults they trust keep saying so. To address this, adults can help teens rewrite their story's MacGuffin by opening the briefcase to show the worthwhile treasure inside.

Re-authoring a MacGuffin starts with awareness of the conflicting goals and examining them. Again, adults can only offer help and guidance, they cannot become the author of the story. If adults are doing most of the talking, then this error is being made. It takes very little prompting to get teens to focus on an examination of their core conflicting beliefs, but it requires not getting lost in tangent thoughts. Keep teens talking about their core thoughts (not peripheral threads), keep them reflecting on the underlying values they're struggling with. Give them space to figure it out and eventually they will create a new priority. Any emotional distress will subside. Of course, sometimes, teens choose a priority that does not correspond to the adults' choice, but trying to advocate in that situation has little chance of success. A better strategy when teens choose the "wrong" priority is to wait for further periods of inevitable distress where re-authoring the current MacGuffins is the teens' imperative, not the adults'.

In most cases, mental focus on underlying values and beliefs quickly prioritizes subconscious goals and helps people feel better

(Carey, 2006). It will still be difficult but they are able to move forward. Superman accepted that he will not kill, even to save Lois. He was devastated to think she would die, but he was no longer paralyzed in acute shock. Most complex choices do not involve such high stakes. So, psychologists and philosophers have devised many thought experiments to further examine the phenomenon. One of the most famous is the "trolley problem." Imagine standing on a train platform. On the tracks below, three people are tied down with a runaway trolley coming toward them and they will be killed. You cannot untie them in time but luckily a switch is nearby, flip this switch to send the train onto a sidetrack and save the three people. Unfortunately, a different person has been tied on that alternative track. So, flipping the switch kills that one person instead. Most people said they would flip the switch, noting that saving three people is more ethical than saving only one. It's a matter of math. When the story is slightly altered most people have a different answer. Imagine that instead of a switch, a large man stands on the platform nearby, you can push him so he falls on the track stopping the trolley with his immense girth and save the three tied up people but kill the man. Do you push the man? Changing the story from "flipping a switch" to "pushing a man" alters many people's answer because they now see the underlying value.

The value at stake was hidden with the "flip the switch" but clear with the "push the man." This value involves personal responsibility. If I'm standing on a track and see a train kill three people who are tied down, I'm not an actor in the story, I'm an observer. The person who set up the situation is the murderer. If I flip the switch, now I am an actor, I am a murderer. It can be justified, but the question is, "Will I be a murderer or not?" Pushing the man in front of the train makes this choice clear. When Batman intervened with Superman he was clarifying the values involved, he was reframing the situation to make it clear what's really going on. Is killing justifiable if it saves others? Now this question can be debated and answered in different ways, that's not the point. The interesting aspect of the "trolley problem" experiment is that most people don't notice the underlying value. They engage a cold utilitarian logic with the "switch" version, but have an emotional realization with the "push." Adults can help teens make the emotional connection, they can illuminate the underlying value choices and highlight the emotional impact of a choice. They cannot make the choice for the teen.

However, even though adults cannot make the choice for the teen, they can make it for themselves. Every mental process that goes on for a child and teen also happens for adults. To be a guide for teens and kids in emotional distress when their values are in paradoxical conflict, adults must not also be in similar emotional distress. Recognizing the value driving an argument, action, or discussion can be just as impactful as helping teens recognize what's going on for them. A common example of parental cognitive dissonance is when the beliefs "My child should like me" and "My child should do what I say" are in play at the same time. Parents often want a "good" relationship with their children. They can accept not being best friends, but warmth, compassion and kindness are expected. This priority is paradoxically opposed by the need to "Make kids be respectful" and the expectation that children "Do what they're told." Pursuing either of these goals can be appropriate, but trying to have both at the same time can cause intense conflicts both inside the adult and interpersonally with the child. As a professional educator and mental healthcare provider, I am able to work with extreme behaviors without getting upset because I have consciously chosen my priority. Often, this is "Do what I say." A commonly uttered phrase in my classroom was, "You don't have to like it, you just have do it." Alternatively, sometimes if a child is in acute emotional distress, my priority is for the child to "calm down." Of course, I can more easily make these choices because of practice and because my relationship with the child is far different than a parent. Still, mastering the art of self-awareness and noticing what MacGuffin is being pursued is within any parent's reach.

The last important aspect of the MacGuffin is that it can't be reached easily. Characters must get a glimpse of it, hear of its legend, or possess it briefly just before it's snatched away. They cannot truly obtain the prize until the trials of the story have been overcome. In movies, the second act of the story is where most of this takes place. This is the space between the hero accepting the quest and when he must make his final push to reach the goal. In this time frame, the hero has many smaller trials, he almost succeeds, and then all hope is lost before he recovers to make a final stand. Accepting this process can be liberating for both parents and kids.

A goal is accomplished through many small steps. In the middle of this second act when taking the next small step, it can feel like no progress is being made. When the inevitable setback occurs, we might feel it was all for nothing. This is of course all part of the story. It's all necessary. Highlighting this fact and the progress already made sounds obvious, but many people get stuck focusing on what hasn't yet been achieved instead of what has. One strategy that's tried and true to help avoid this tendency is the creation of a formal plan. Writing down broad goals, short term objectives and regular progress is a tool that is used universally. However, it can be difficult to stick to it. Indeed, the process has tremendous power, yet can be easily put aside in the light of the most current crisis. Many types of professionals are paid to implement this process for others, with some companies paying top dollar to managers who can keep progress towards goals moving efficiently, within budget, and on time. Parents can help teens by first mastering this process for themselves and then modeling the skill for the teen. Young children can even be taught directly. In the end, it can help to keep in mind that a MacGuffin (goal) is necessary for the story, but it's the journey to that goal, all the small steps of the second act that make up the bulk of the story. So enjoy the process, because a new goal will be waiting soon.

5

LIFE: THE SEQUEL

"It wasn't as good as the first one." This phrase has been uttered by countless moviegoers after viewing that strange creation, the sequel. The golden goose of Hollywood is the "franchise," a series of movies about a single character or world. These are goldmines because each entry into the franchise has a built in audience. Of course, the real money from franchises is in the merchandising, but toys and clothes cannot exist if no new films are released. Sequels can be talked about for years before being released. They are debated on the internet, spies try to get glimpses of the scripts, and casting is bet on in Las Vegas. Sequels can open with massive numbers worldwide. And yet, when the movie fails to be as good as the original, no one is surprised. We all know that catching lightning in a bottle twice is unlikely. Why then is there such a fervor around sequels?

Sequels carry an inevitable paradox. When a movie or story is great, we the audience never want it to end. The chance to see our favorite characters again and revisit the magical places we grew to cherish is a fantastic opportunity. However, the reason we love a story is because it's a good one, it has all the critical components of a good story. One of those basic pieces is the transformation of the hero. In Joseph Campbell's (1968) analysis, this is when the hero returns from the "underworld" with an "elixir." The underworld is the special world of the story that the character must enter. The elixir is the change the character needed, the remedy to the pathos that has plagued him throughout the story. We the audience know that going forward things will be better for our hero, he can now succeed in places he failed before completing the adventure. Again, this transformation is critical for most stories to work and connect with audiences. If the story is continued in a sequel, then we begin where the old story left off. Our hero is already transformed. The reason the first story was great is because it was centered on the hero's outer and inner journey. The outer journey can be replicated easily with similar but different enough settings, antagonists, etc. The inner journey is not so simple. How can it be replicated? We already saw the inner change in the first story yet we all want the same story over again. We loved the first story, but if it's replicated with only slight changes it doesn't make sense. Of course, we don't inherently know any of these technical reasons, we just feel let down because something that was in the first story was left out of the second.

This expectation of transformation after an adventure has many implications in how parents and children interact. Many adults working with children and teens have the inherent expectation that growth and change is a linear progression as this generally makes basic sense. A person learns a new skill, practices that skill and eventually masters it. It's believed that a similar process happens for children as they grow; children struggle with problems, have epiphanies and learn how to solve those problems. If similar situations occur again, the children can easily handle them. For example, in the movie *Ghostbusters* (Reitman, 1984), four paranormal investigators discover the secret to tracking and catching ghosts. They build a successful business around their discovery and eventually win over the naysayers by saving the entire city from a giant rampaging Marshmallow Man. The main character, Dr. Peter Venkman, portrayed by Bill Murray, has an obvious character flaw.

He's a selfish opportunist. He begins the movie exploiting a research project to get a date, and his motivation to catch ghosts centers on becoming rich, not saving the city. Through the story he changes. He realizes the error of his ways when he develops strong feelings for a woman who doesn't fall for his tricks. Dr. Venkman finds he is willing to sacrifice himself to save the city and become the person he previously pretended to be. In the final moments of the film, he and the other Ghostbusters perform a maneuver they believe will take out the monster but also kill themselves. They inexplicably survive and we leave the story confident that Dr. Venkman has learned his lesson, he will marry the woman he loves and the Ghostbusters will continue to defend the city. When *Ghostbusters II* was released, audiences found their expectations were far from realized (Reitman, 1989). The sequel found our heroes fallen from grace, no longer in business, and legally restrained from ghost hunting. Furthermore, the woman Dr. Venkman had pursued throughout the first movie had married someone else. The sequel takes us through identical steps (known as "beats" in movie lingo). The characters start in the same place they began the first movie. Dr. Venkman is exploiting people on a talk show and is in the same selfish space as before. The movie doesn't score well with audiences even though it's almost identical to the first. This is because audiences want to see bigger and better adventures from the characters as we, the audience, expect them to continue the linear growth trajectory.

In reality, the story of many people is more like *Ghostbusters II* than we realize. This is due to a phenomenon normally called regression. When a person practices and improves a skill, the line of improvement is far from straight. In experiments, improvement is tracked on an X and Y axis; for example X is the score and Y is time. On a scale of 100, a child might score 50 at first, the next day with tutoring and practice they score 55, the following they score 60, but the fourth day they score 45. Many adults get extraordinarily frustrated when this occurs, and may accuse the child of "not trying" or "slacking." The tutoring might be doubled and the child then scores a 55. The adult breathes a sigh of relief, they've lost ground but now improvement has returned. The next score, 48. This is happening because improvement in the real world has many factors and occurs over a long period of time in small non-linear increments. Again, this doesn't feel right. The subconscious assumption is, "People learn and move forward, they have an epiphany and never repeat the mistake." This belief is seen in the stories we tell. When the story deviates, like in sequels, we don't like it. In real life, a regression can create extreme frustration and anger. Adults may become irate with children who don't progress in a straightforward fashion and make all kinds of assumptions about that lack of progress. The truth is that people are messy and will rarely progress in a straight line (Ariely, 2010; Kahneman, 2015).

Many adults get tricked by the regression phenomenon into thinking that harsh criticism is the best training strategy. They are not alone - the "drill instructor" is the iconic representation of this mentality. Many parents/teachers support the "drill instructor" mentality because of the following type of scenario. A student is given a task and achieves a measurable score (good or maybe bad). The same task tried the next day is worse than the first and the adult proceeds to yell and scream insults at the student. Amazingly, the student does better the next day and the adult thinks that the yelling helped and gives the student praise for raising the score. However, the next practice session results in regression to a lower score. To the adult, the lower score simply reaffirms that the yelling should have continued instead of any praise What's happening is known as "regression towards the mean." Mean in this case is the average of scores over a long period of time. As the student attempts to improve he will score around that average. The tendency will be to move up and down around the average as one day the score will be higher than average and then soon there will be a day with a below average score. Over time, given enough practice, the average will go up and there will be significant growth from the start of training and the end of training. The problem is that this growth cannot be seen on a daily basis. It feels like no progress is being made, like we're just replaying the same movie over and over again with slightly different settings (Ariely, 2010; Kahneman, 2015).

A common formula for a sequel is to send our characters to new places. The same story takes place but the hope is that the new settings will make it interesting. In the *Die Hard* series, each movie finds our hero against terrorists in varying locales, but the story is always about our "everyman" hero and his sidekicks against overwhelming odds (Silver, Gordon, & McTiernan, 1988). Indiana Jones was looking for a Judeo-Christian relic in the Middle East and Europe, so in the sequel we'll send him to India to search for Hindu relics (Watts & Spielberg, 1984). In *Star Wars,* the story begins on a desert planet, the sequel starts on an ice planet (Kurtz & Kershner, 1980). Usually, this doesn't work so well, and the audience still feels the movie is less than the original because the story is the same. It's assumed that when a hero enters a "new world" that the hero will be challenged to change for the better and if faced with the same problem in a different setting, the hero should be able to handle it easily due to a grand inner change. When the hero enters the new world in a sequel but simply goes through identical transformations it doesn't feel right.

Interestingly, in reality, a slight change in setting can prompt a whole new story arc. For example, in extreme cases, children can be sent to inpatient settings where they live at a treatment center. In this setting, a great deal of time, effort and patience goes into achieving long term changes. These improvements are clearly documented and explained. However, many parents are frustrated and confused because when the child returns home it is as if no change had occurred. They thought the child's inner journey change that took place in the inpatient center would be permanent and in place when the child came home. Why didn't that happen? In reality, it's hardwired into our storytelling mind that the child must now go through a new journey to change while being part of the family. This truth is counter-intuitive and frustrating because it means that all the work and pain must take place in the family system with everyone involved. It's not a disease that can be cured through a "treatment." Parents can save a great deal of heartache by accepting the nature of regression and the fact that their child's hero's journey must occur over and over again in different settings. No grand transformation will make them "better" in all places.

An alternative method in making a sequel is continuing the story with a new quest to change a different pathos. In the time traveling adventure *Back to the Future*, the hero Marty must reunite his parents after mucking up their timeline when he accidentally travels to 1955 (Canton, Gale, & Zemeckis, 1985). In the process, he must overcome his simplistic and arrogant view of his parents as "losers" and comes to appreciate them as people with their own flaws and dreams. In learning this acceptance, he unknowingly creates a new brighter future where his parents had their own inner transformation that cascaded through time. In making the sequel, the producers wisely knew this nuanced inner arc could not easily be repeated so instead the producers created a new pathos. Unfortunately, this new inner flaw that must be conquered was simplistic and contrived, simply being that Marty hated being called a "coward." Although this flaw was not seen in the first movie and didn't make much sense, there was a need for a new inner journey.

A more successful version of this tactic is *Star Wars: The Empire Strikes Back* (Kurtz & Kershner, 1980). In the first film, Luke

Skywalker must trust in himself and his potential. He takes action to overcome his simplistic mindset and learns to trust in his own abilities. He ends the film as a heroic soldier who saved the princess and destroyed the enemy base. In the sequel, Luke seems to be continuing his journey towards becoming a Jedi, a space samurai with mystical powers. Luke's struggle centers on sacrifices necessary to achieve this goal. He is tested when he must choose to sacrifice his friends if he is to continue in his training. In the climax of the film, Luke's inner struggle further crystallizes with the revelation that the evil Darth Vader is actually his father. Luke is tempted with the promise of absolute power and reunification with his long lost parent. His transformation occurs when he makes the ultimate sacrifice to reject Darth Vader's offer and drop into an abyss, knowing that he will most likely not survive. Luckily, his friends, who he came to help, end up saving him.

In both of these examples, the story of our hero is expanded due to new inner conflicts. Marty's in *Back to the Future* didn't work because it was too simple and seemed tacked on just to make another movie. *The Empire Strikes Back* works so well because the next inner challenge for Luke seemed to be an organic consequence of the first movie. In life, the end of one story arc is the beginning of a new one. No living person is devoid of a story arc. Living "happily ever after" is a phrase that has no substance. The next story might make a "genre" switch and become a light comedy with small stakes or a huge epic with life threatening stakes, but a story exists because people are part of it.

The notion that children move from one story arc to another while often having many stories occurring at the same time is something that parents can work to accept. But, some parents and children become disheartened and depressed when they work towards a goal, achieve it, only to be confronted by a new goal - acing the midterm moves on to trying to ace the final. They win the state championship but now must go to nationals. The never-ending external goal can feel repetitive and unfulfilling, but using each new external challenge to overcome other internal challenges can create a sense of fulfillment. Focusing on how new goals create opportunities for further inner growth and transformation can change a boring *Ghostbusters II* sequel into the hailed *Empire Strikes Back*.

How can this be accomplished? While we might not be the author of the story and choose all of our conflicts, we can be more than just the player, more than just the actor. As a director shapes a story written by another, we can shape our story to focus on anything we like. To exemplify this point, consider George Lucas, the creator of *Star Wars*. For much of the history of *Star Wars*, he has maintained that a grand story arc existed and that he set out the long-term character arc when writing the first film. This is not true at all. Many documented sources including original script drafts, notes, recorded interviews, and meeting transcripts all clearly show that no grand story existed. After *Star Wars* was a hit, Lucas set out to create a sequel. He realized that something needed to change in order to make the sequel different and meaningful. "What if Darth Vader was Luke's father?" became the basis of a whole new pathos for Luke. That seemed pretty cool; however, there were problematic issues at shoehorning in this new story element. For example, it turned the Obi Wan character into a strange manipulative liar when he told Luke in the first movie that Darth Vader betrayed and murdered his father. This was dealt with using (some pretty thin) wordplay and rationalization when he told Luke he was speaking from a "certain point of view." The new Darth Vader father angle worked great with other aspects of the first film. When Luke's uncle worries that Luke has "too much of his father in him," he is no longer worrying Luke will run off to join the military to get killed. He is now making an ominous forecast that Luke has potential for great evil. By adding this single element, George Lucas transformed the story arc of the first movie and made room for a new compelling inner arc in the sequel (Kaminski, 2008).

Parents can help children and teens use the same tactic by adding a new meaningful inner goal to the current external task which can make all the difference emotionally. In my classroom, a typical use of this method grew from students' need to complete repetitive academic tasks. They often would come into the school failing primarily due to not completing assignments. With lots of individualized support, they would begin to improve. My initial method to keep them moving forward was to frame the initial internal struggle around "perseverance" and the ability to tolerate the pain of boredom to complete tasks. After this was mastered, students would begin asking to transfer back to the "normal" school. In most cases, parents and district administrators would not consider a transfer unless a long duration of success was recorded. Students would become disheartened that they could not use effort to progress faster, they could only continue to use the perseverance skills they already mastered. As the teacher, my job was to re-write this sequel story to include a new inner journey, usually built around "self-control." The external goal changed from not only completing tasks but completing tasks without adult reminders or help. This of course was standard practice in the school program but the trick to success was getting the student to buy into the new inner journey, that they must overcome a new pathos by completing the assignments solo.

Yet another aspect of the sequel story is the raising of stakes. In the groundbreaking *Lensmen* book series, E.E. Smith helped create an entirely new genre, the "Space Opera" (Smith, 1950). First written in 1937, these were a series of stories about policeman versus gangsters. The twist was setting the story in space with intricate descriptions of amazing futuristic technology and alien worlds. Each story arc set the hero against an evil organization that, at first, were simply galactic drug smugglers, but in each installment the giant scope and reach of this evil grew. The powers and means of the heroes also grew in proportion to face the expanding threat. In the end, laser battles between spaceships escalated into hurling entire planets. As each story arc concluded in defeating the enemy, a discovery of the "true" villain was made. Each sequel required a quest for a new means to overcome this new "true" evil, but of course at the end of the next story another "true" enemy was revealed. If the grand scope of the evil empire had been seen at the beginning of the series, then the hero would believe there was no chance of winning. In each installment, the hero faced a great adversary but one that was within reach of defeating.

In education and psychology, this is called "scaffolding," to break large tasks into smaller understandable bits. This is not new or profound. The interesting aspect of the *Lensman* series is the growth that the character takes in facing each level of the antagonist organization. The hero takes pride and satisfaction in each new insight and progression. Many adults scoff at the notion of giving children participation awards or celebrating small achievements, but these milestones are the closing of one story and the beginning of another. As the child glimpses the next even grander challenge awaiting them, they can remember the previous adventure and build on that success. Again, this is about emotional satisfaction of one story being completed and a new story being created that is just as meaningful and exciting as the previous one. In the end, focusing on the inner journey of each story arc aids not only in success with the outer goal but also makes the whole journey a lot more fun.

6

ENTER THE LOVE INTEREST

The "Love Interest" is an interesting aspect of any story. As humans, we strive for connection and companionship. We are social animals that create stories centered in a social sphere. In terms of story, the love interest can come in several flavors. Recognizing the "love interest" in your teens' life can be a great benefit in both understanding their actions and helping to guide them through the process.

First, a word on sex and the power of attraction. Many parents struggle with the topic of sex and how/when to have the infamous "birds and the bees" discussion. The topic of sex is taboo in many cultures and yet in western society it's front and center in obvious ways. Specific values around sex are beyond the scope of this book, but the power that sex has over every individual's story to a greater or lesser degree is undeniable. Whether the story is framed around meeting a "soul mate" to get married and have a family or simply to "score" with the object of desire, both involve the physical drive in people to copulate and reproduce.

For many years, I was the instructor of the 8th grade "health" class at my special education school. Our eighth graders were considerably more emotionally immature than typical kids, many with autism diagnoses. However, their education plans specified standard curriculum with only accommodations to help them learn, so health class (really sex ed) was required. While I was never the primary middle school teacher, I was often called in whenever a difficult situation arose that the normal teacher felt they couldn't handle. I didn't blame them, it was extraordinarily hard. To give an example, the state approved curriculum focused on sexually transmitted diseases, the failure rate of condoms, and the adoption of abstinence as the best method of avoiding STDs. After carefully planned and implemented lessons, the boys could demonstrate a basic understanding of the concepts, at least right after the lesson. Invariably, when they arrived the next day, the ideas had strangely morphed in their minds into something like: "If I wear a condom and kiss a girl, she'll be pregnant, and I'll have an STD." Getting the basic facts straight was difficult enough, but there was also the emotional concepts that could simply be out of reach for many of the students. However, even with the confusion, what was especially interesting was the drive that many of these students had towards relationships. They didn't understand exactly what they were feeling, but it was powerful. Sometimes, the outward signs were easy to spot, like when a boy sits and stares obsessively at a young female assistant teacher. Alternatively, the signs could be obtuse, like when an autistic boy asked a female teacher to let him inspect her teeth. These boys had physical and emotional urges that came out in some way. For teens, "romantic love" is an integral part of the story and often the center of the story. This is common knowledge and no great revelation, but for many parents understanding exactly how the love interest fits into their teens' heroic story can be of great help.

When *Superman* was first created by Jerry Siegel and Joe Shuster, the authors were still in their teens. They envisioned a stronger than life hero to take on the problems of their day such as crooked politicians and gangsters. They borrowed heavily (some might say "stole") from the stories that inspired them. Some aspects of these "inspirations" were borrowed in detailed ways, like from Edgar Rice Burroughs' *A Princess of Mars* where a man (John Carter) on a smaller alien planet would have superior strength compared to natives due to the difference in gravity. Superman's strength and speed on Earth versus his home planet of Krypton was directly analogous to John Carter's strength on Mars versus Earth. What didn't get ported over was the complex character of Dejah Thoris, the love interest in the John Carter story. The complexities of the strong female ally were lost and what remained in the Superman story was a surface character, simply a damsel in distress to be rescued. As the love interest of Superman, Lois Lane was what the male teen authors wanted, an attractive woman to rescue and get attention from. For many years in the early days of *Superman* comics, Lois was treated in terribly misogynistic ways. Only later did she transform slowly into a more complex character (Tye, 2013).

The "damsel in distress" motif is pervasive and the starting point for most young male stories. The original *Wonder Woman* stories were of particular interest because of the purposeful way they went against this trend, where the love interest had a complex relationship with the heroine. Of course, later in *Wonder Woman's* run after creator William Marston was no longer the writer, the old pattern re-emerged with Steve Trevor becoming an object for Wonder Woman to rescue (Hanley, 2014). The love interest becomes the MacGuffin, the goal of the story. From classic fairy tales like *Snow White* to video games like *Super Mario Bros.*, the love interest as goal is where many teens begin their story.

Rescuing the princess often works fine for a while, as young boys and girls don't need anything more complex. As people mature, something changes in the way a love interest interweaves into the story. Many people are unaware that this change has occurred. They see a movie or read a story with a basic "save the girl" plot and feel let down. However, viewing another movie that on the surface is the same (a girl is rescued) "feels" better, but the reason for the difference is not obvious. The change comes in how the love interest works directly in the hero's journey, in the transformation of the protagonist.

In *The Matrix*, a young computer programmer named Neo discovers that the world is actually a giant computer program and reality is a post-apocalyptic hell-scape ruled by robots. All humanity is enslaved in a virtual prison they don't even know exists. However, Neo begins this epic adventure by simply following the love interest, Trinity. Trinity is a woman working with human freedom fighters searching for a mythical savior known as "The One." Neo is a candidate for this title but doesn't believe it at first. He is focused on the girl. Neo's character arc centers on his acceptance that he is "The One." The growth towards this character change is mirrored in his relationship with Trinity. As he is filled with total doubt, Trinity is aloof. As Neo changes to consider the possibility, Trinity grows to be flirtatious. As Neo rejects the idea, Trinity becomes irritated. When Neo finally accepts his role, it's in conjunction with Trinity's revelation that she can only fall in love with "The One." Since Neo has earned her love through self-sacrifice, he must be the long sought savior. Beat for beat, the closeness of their relationships mirrors the hero's journey and the internal character arc (Silver, Wachowski & Wachowski, 1999).

This is not limited to a few movies or stories, but rather is hardwired into most stories. When it is absent, the story may still work, but often feels incomplete. For many teens (and adults), the story they are living centers on solidifying a relationship. At the basic level, it's driven by biological urges to save the princess. However, this is later overladen with a drive to achieve a full relationship that is more meaningful. Teens will talk about "falling in love" with someone and do all kinds of strange things to "earn" the other's love. In their story, obtaining their love "target" will result in a feeling of catharsis, that they have achieved something special, that they themselves have become something better. This is what a good love story will replicate, a feeling of transcendental lightness. Of course, as stated earlier, once the story is over, a new one needs to begin. The teens have a conflict and break up, only to get back together or pursue a new person. They're seeking that feeling of transformation that comes with a "true" love.

Parents and adults can help teens in their "hero's journey" as the love interest may or may not be taking center stage. The situation can get quite confusing as the underlying feelings and beliefs get intertwined with all aspects of the story. It's not uncommon for teens to believe that obtaining some external goal is directly connected to achieving a relationship with the love interest, such as, "If I get on the football team, the girl will like me." All kinds of goals are tied up with the love interest and strange behaviors often result as teens try to reach a specific goal with absolute belief that it will lead to success with the girl/boy love interest. This confusion is a result of not consciously understanding that achieving the external goal and forming a relationship with that special person are both outgrowths of the internal character arc. Remember, character arcs center on values, beliefs and expectations. This can be the focus of adult interventions. Trying to rationalize with teens through logical arguments will often do little to shape their behavior. They will often genuinely agree with ideas and arguments posed by adults, but the feelings that come up when the hero's journey calls are unbearable. They must be addressed.

Asking teens to describe their values, beliefs and expectations can be a good starting point. Often the conversation starts with the simple external goal that's causing problems; they got cut from the football team, they didn't make the pep squad, etc. Then, asking questions to discover what these events meant to the story of the teen will often reveal the love interest connection. As a matter of practice, when working with boys especially, I always assume a love interest is in play. Simple questions such as, "What did Jenny say about you not making the football team?" can get to that deeper level. Often a burst of emotion occurs when this connection is exposed and the teens seem angry. But this is just embarrassment and an adult can play it cool to keep the conversation going. Again, the key is remembering that to teens it's all connected, "Becoming a better person," "Having a good future," "Getting a date with Jenny," and "Making the football team" can all be the same at the emotional story level. Helping teenagers realize the underlying beliefs, values, and expectations at play is often the best (and sometimes only) thing an adult can do to help teens move in a positive direction.

Of course, the "love interest" doesn't need to be a romantic interest. In the movie *Hot Fuzz*, superstar policeman Nicholas Angel is transferred from the big city to a small country town. This is because he is a great policeman but he has emotionally isolated everyone in his life. In fact, he is unable to keep a relationship because of his single-minded devotion to being the "best" police officer. In his new position, he is confronted with a situation in which his "by the book" obsession not only isolates him emotionally but also keeps him from uncovering a massive conspiracy. At the beginning of the story, Nicholas is partnered with Danny, a goofball policeman who has his job through nepotism. As Nicholas is forced to uncover the mystery, he is also able to make a transformation in himself to see that there is more to life than being "the best." He comes to embrace the adventurous and joyful aspects of his life. As this change progresses, the relationship between Nicholas and Danny grows ever closer. In the end, the two become true partners and friends, with both enjoying each other's company and appreciating the skills they bring to the job. This is an example of the "Buddy Comedy" or the "Bromance" (Bevan, Fellner, Park & Wright, 2007).

The "Buddy" story is a variation on the love interest. The same underlying emotional components are in play. As the hero changes internally and gets closer to his external goals, the relationship with the buddy blossoms. The story culminates with feelings of catharsis as friends consolidate the emotional connection. Adults can often see this happening in the stories of children as they become obsessed with a particular friend. The same strategies of focusing on underlying values, beliefs, and expectations can be just as useful when a child or teen is in crisis over a friendship. The adult can remember that the feeling of "losing" the friend is the same as failing in the whole story. They have lost everything, because in the hero's story, the friendship is in proportion to success in the story. None of this is true in the cold sense of "reality" but the reason a movie without a romantic love interest (or a bromance) feels strange is because we feel strange without these interpersonal connections.

Social interaction is hardwired and comes out in every way possible. In the movie *Castaway*, the love interest is a volleyball that becomes the only friend of a man stranded on a deserted island (Hanks, Rapke, Starkey & Zemeckis, 2000). We the audience grow to believe in the relationship and see the volleyball as a character. We feel terrible distress when it is lost, just as young children will be in complete meltdown when a particular stuffed animal is lost.

The need for social connection can be an all-powerful compulsion that many children and teens cannot ignore. Most kids master subtle ways to communicate in order to maintain the story that many adults expect. Specifically, adults often live by the old idea that "Children are to be seen, not heard." It's amazing how pervasive this idea is.

Many adults profess to wanting to foster children's social growth but also have a hard time letting kids communicate in any way they want. Indeed, the majority of schools are inherently designed to keep children quietly engaged in "school work." Teachers' effectiveness is often judged by how quiet children are kept in the room. Therefore, complex systems of rewards and punishments are created to maintain quiet order. Yet, in all the movies and stories that take place in schools and classrooms, rarely is there a scene in which students quietly write. Kids in these stories find ways to send notes, whisper or engage in some other method of communication. The relationship is how the story progresses and this pull towards progression is incredible for all people. It's an old joke that teachers make the worst students, and in my experience, a group of teachers is not going to sit quietly without engaging in some type of interpersonal communication any more than kids are.

Does this mean kids and teens should be allowed to communicate whenever they want? Not at all, but it does mean we shouldn't be surprised by the extreme measure that kids and teens will take to keep the story going and make connections with other people. Adults must understand that keeping children and teens quietly isolated is not a natural way of being, it's not the way they are going to feel good about their progress in the story of life. They can be taught to endure it, to tolerate it, but for the most part, they will not like it. Again, this is okay, but understanding what's going on is the key to adults using effective interventions without emotionally reacting themselves.

A final complication with the love interest in our personal story is that of the "lust" interest. In many stories, a hero focuses on engaging a relationship with a certain person because that person is physically attractive, popular, rich, or has some other superficial quality that is desirable. As the story progresses, this type of person is pursued. However, unlike a regular love interest, as the hero changes internally and grows emotionally, it becomes clear that the original object of desire is not actually what the hero wants. The "true" love interest is the friend or other person who was not considered by the hero as a "love interest" until the hero's internal transformation occurred.

In *Teen Wolf*, a young high schooler named Scott Howard, played by Michael J. Fox, has an obsessive crush on the beautiful popular girl, Pamela. When he finds out that he can transform into a werewolf and thus obtain superhuman powers, he begins a quest to form a relationship with her. He becomes a basketball star because of the implied connection that this external goal will equate to the desired relationship. As the story progresses, Pamela is revealed to be shallow and vapid, while the true love interest is the childhood best friend named Boof. In the end, after the hero realizes he doesn't need to cheat with superpowers to win the basketball game because his integrity is more important than winning, he also realizes that he has true romantic feelings for Boof (Levinson & Daniel, 1985).

This phenomenon in the story feels satisfying to the audience, and it feels satisfying in life. Many people have experienced the pursuit of a relationship or other goal only to realize after an internal change that the goal was not desired anymore. Stories show this effect constantly and it can act as a safeguard in many situations. Adults using the technique of asking teens questions that dig to the underlying beliefs, values and expectations can subtly highlight how an object of desire is not the true love interest but just a part of the journey. Again, helping teens realize this takes subtlety. However, even with the best of intentions to be subtle, adults often just point out all of the flaws of the "lust" interest and then conclude with, "If he doesn't like you, he's an idiot and not good enough." This tactic of telling teens directly is usually not as effective as coaxing it out of them through questions.

> **Parent:** "I'm just curious, what did he do to win your devotion?"
>
> **Daughter:** "He's really nice."
>
> **Parent:** "Oh, I see. Is he nicer than all the other boys?"
>
> **Daughter:** "Yeah."
>
> **Parent:** "So what did he do that was so nice? Did he defend you from bullies or something?"
>
> **Daughter:** "No, not like that, he's just nice."
>
> **Parent:** "Oh, OK...but you're not sure exactly why?"

This kind of questioning can help teens break the spell of the story they are in and shift the focus to their internal growth. Highlighting this growth lays the foundation for feeling renewed to find the "true" love interest. The idea of "true love" can be a double-edged sword and lead teens to all kinds of poor choices in the name of "love." Focusing on values and beliefs helps frame true love in terms of the person who matches those beliefs. Achieving a relationship with a person who matches one's inner growth results in in the feeling of catharsis that we are all looking for, the feeling we have after seeing a good romantic movie.

7

I HAVE THE POWER

Popular stories through the ages are great ways to discover a group's or culture's mainstream beliefs about various aspects of life. Specific themes and character arcs that are revisited many times by different authors can show the pervasiveness of certain ideas. These small aspects around particular ideas that constantly pop up in stories are known as "tropes." These elements are not the focus of the story or the message that the author wants to convey. They are patterns that sneak into a story, many times without the author's direct awareness. These mental constructs are so ingrained in the society of the author and audience that they're often barely noticed. All kinds of tropes have been used through the millennia of storytelling culture. They can be categorized in many ways and databases of thousands of popular tropes can be found easily on the internet. There is one trope in particular called the "object of power" that illustrates an underlying belief that is widespread in our culture and impacts the lives of children and teens.

In many ancient stories, a warrior may be wielding a fantastic weapon. This weapon may have been handed down a family line and provides a great advantage to the wielder. In the epic story, the sword might be described as "Craving the blood of the enemy." It's an exciting phrase, but there's a more robust concept underneath. The idea is that objects, weapons, tools, plants, and people all have a metaphysical force, a vitality that fuels them and guides their progress in the story. A sword that has its own goals and desires is just one version. One of the most famous vitalistic weapons in epic story history is Excalibur, the sword of King Arthur. The stories of King Arthur date back to the dark ages, but most aspects that we know today are composed of many layers of additions from over the centuries (Shippey, 2015). In 1981, the movie simply named *Excalibur* traces the history of the sword as it's passed from a mystical "Lady of the Lake" to the Wizard Merlin, then to King Uther, and then finally to Uther's son King Arthur (Boorman, 1981). The sword possesses unheard-of strength and it's the envy of the other knights, as it proves Arthur as the true king and enables him to conquer all of England. The historicity of the Arthurian legend is not as important as the lasting impact that the stories have had through the ages. The idea of a sword of power that has innate special qualities remains appealing today. This can be seen in new versions of the King Arthur story being produced continuously. In everyday life, many people have experienced the passing of a special object from generation to generation - their own version of "Excalibur."

The item of power, the totem, the representation of a desired quality like courage, strength, or wisdom is so commonplace in our stories that it barely registers as a "thing." When Luke is given his father's lightsaber in *Star Wars*, it just makes sense (Kurtz & Lucas, 1977). When Harry Potter is given the twin wand of Voldemort, it makes sense (Rowling, 1997). These acts further develop the heroes' stories by solidifying their connection to the past and foreshadowing their adventure to come. Children and teens (and adults) constantly embody objects in their lives with a kind of special power and meaning. Having an object of power can produce feelings of calmness, confidence and enthusiasm. This is something that people do without thinking, although it takes concerted effort to notice it happening. I've experienced extremes of this phenomenon when children displayed what is usually called "hoarding" behaviors. They collect specific objects that have some kind of special meaning, then another, and another until whatever storage they use is filled to the brim with all manner of objects, many of which adults would classify as trash. I have also worked with adult hoarders which is more difficult in some ways because learning new ways of self-soothing and recreating the feeling that comes from all the "precious" objects can be more challenging after 20 years of practicing hoarding versus children with only one year of doing such.

Understanding the inevitability of this phenomenon can help parents intervene when necessary and in ways that will be most beneficial. Classically, cultures have exploited the act of passing down special objects throughout the history of humanity. The impact of this act to a child's story is well known and celebrated in all manner of rituals and ceremonies. Many of these are still performed throughout the world today and come in all shapes and sizes and may be religious, secular, ethnic, or familial. Unfortunately, many kids and teens may not see "specialness" of the thing meant to be the object of power in the same way adults see it. Parents may give a child a family heirloom with great gravitas and ceremony only to find it's been lost a week later. The objects that kids and teens hold dear must be chosen by them because these items become characters in their stories. However, an adult can help create this character so it has a positive impact to the story. The item might provide soothing during times of distress and confidence in times of pressure as opposed to a negative impact where the object becomes overbearing, a source of anxiety if lost, or an obsessive need to collect similar objects.

For kids on the autism spectrum, collecting a specific type of object can become all-consuming. Unlike an obsessive compulsive hoarder, an autistic child or teen may not see any problem with their furious need to collect, watch, or discuss the special object. I have worked with teens who exhibited all manner of object obsessions, and the focus on specific objects invariably changes over time. One boy focused on hot peppers and hot sauces, while he later became focused on pizza toppings, and still later on sandwiches. Many teen boys were focused on popular characters from cartoons and video games, characters whose stories they wanted to reproduce. Some focused on machinery like garbage trucks, tractors, motorcycles, etc. Adults must understand the importance of the "power objects", the inevitability of there being such objects, and the difficulties that can arise.

Armed with this understanding, what kinds of interventions can adults employ when confronting extreme situations, such as with autism and hoarding? What are the alternatives when traditional ceremonial approaches don't take? The first step is always being aware that these items of power are extraordinarily important to the child's story, it's their Excalibur. It is the source of their strength, and it's a part of who they are. Separating children from the object may produce all types of anxiety, even panic attacks. For example, I once worked with an elderly man who struggled with hoarding and vomited in my office due to anxiety because he was being forced to get rid of certain pieces of furniture. It would have been easy for me to be judgmental and classify this overreaction as attention-seeking or some other demeaning description. I had to remember that for him this pain was real, that it was okay to be in pain, and it was a necessary step to moving forward so I was compassionate and understanding. My role was not to take away his pain but to help him accept that for practical reasons he had to let go of some of the furniture and to make peace with that. Teens can have a similar reaction. I have seen teens react with extreme emotional outpouring for being "grounded" from a computer. They might scream in blood-curdling cries for hours or rage in a violent outburst throwing chairs.

Many adults would classify this as simple "manipulation," which it is, but it's also much more. To the teen who lost the computer, he was losing his friends, the portal into the world in which he felt good about himself. The computer and its programs of connectivity and story were part of his identity. The pain of losing those was immense.

The power that comes from the object is the power that the story places in it. However, it's also how the hero decides to embrace that power. When Luke loses his lightsaber at the end of *Empire Strikes Back* during a fight with his father Darth Vader, it was part of his rejection of Darth Vader and his father's path. In the following movie, *Return of the Jedi*, Luke has created a new lightsaber, one of a different color, one that is completely his own. This story sees Luke honoring his past but also forging a new story of his own choosing, embracing a lightsaber of new green color, different from his father. He later stands up to his father, rejecting the dark side (Kazanjian & Marquand, 1983). Helping children and teens see that their story is more than just the object is the key. They need to learn that the object is a character but not the whole story. They can understand that having a powerful tool can be a great asset but it's not the entirety of a character's strength.

For me, the best method to aid kids and teens around a precious object is asking questions about the item's place in their story. What does the object represent? How does it affect them, the hero? What "powers" does it endow? What feelings come from not having the object? Is there an object of desire that they believe will fix how they feel and give them the power they want? All these types of questions bring the story to the surface and shine light on the emotional content of the object. Over time, kids and teens can be guided in how they incorporate objects of power so they are a source of strength instead of potential foci of obsession. Avoiding the pitfall that thinking happiness lies in obtaining that certain dress, car, or house starts by training kids about the power of objects and the way to harness that power correctly.

As in many situations, pain is unavoidable and an important part of the journey. Feeling the pain of loss when not getting access to a desired object of power can be intense. As we've said, the object represents something profound, a part of the hero, an ally that never lets you down. In order to help children face intense emotional pain, the best tried and true strategy is exposure over time. The idea of gradual exposure is nothing new and seems too simple to be effective. Indeed, exposure therapy is dressed up in all kinds of ways with strange and interesting gimmicks to sell it as more effective than the basic version. But, it all comes down to the basic idea of facing pain directly in small enough doses where a tolerance strategy can be used to keep from going into panic. Over time, the intensity of the pain is increased as the person's tolerance increases. With kids, giving them tools to tolerate the exposure can be helpful as well as keeping the exposure doses at a level where tolerance takes effort but is within reach. I've given kids timers or distractions to help them through it. Sometimes with teens it can be best to front-load them with the importance of facing the pain and make it a type of challenge, like they are training in Kung Fu. Still, in other instances, safety requires a kind of "rapid detox" where the child must face the emotional pain of losing the object and be allowed to rage or tantrum until they can work through it. The adult's job is to validate the child's/teen's pain, to show compassion while still implementing the necessary exposure intervention. For whatever reason, many adults find it easier to do this with young children who scream for hours than with teens who yell profanities and hurl insults. The adult focus must be on keeping cool and knowing that the pain of loss is part of the story, a trial that must be endured. It's not something to take as a personal attack.

Another aspect of the "object of power" trope is passing it down to later generations. This idea can also be seen in the Arthurian legends, as Arthur is the true King of England because his father was not the humble lord he grew up with, but was in fact Uther Pendragon, King of England. In some versions, including most modern retellings, pulling Excalibur from the stone was proof of his heritage (Malory & Rhys, 1906; White, 1958). This of course is just an example of the ancient belief in the power of "bloodlines." This version of vitalism holds that some special metaphysical power is transferred down family lines. In Western culture, this is usually called "nobility." However, the idea that children carry on a family tradition and heritage is seen across cultures and throughout history. Having an heir to carry the power of a bloodline has led many historical characters down dark turns; just think of Henry the VIII and his habit of killing his wives in the quest for a son.

In many ways, the concept of nobility is challenged in modern culture based on enlightenment age thinking that led to modern democracies. The idea that certain families should rule and have authority in government has been highly criticized and most people would not vote to return to a pure aristocracy. However, the underlying belief that some families, some "bloodlines" have special superiority is still pervasive, but of course, the "specialness" may only be recognized by the family members themselves.

Examining the *Harry Potter* story reveals paradoxical implementation of the trope. First, Harry has an Arthurian revelation that he is the inheritor of magical powers and has a place as a hero in a magical world. Throughout the story, the audience is time and time again reminded about Harry's heritage and his need to carry on his parent's legacy. Harry is seen as special, as "the chosen one," and yet the story also vilifies the idea of "pure blood" wizards promoted by the evil wizard Voldemort. In the end, the story falls into the traditional Robin Hood pattern of requiring the hero to be of noble blood who must use his power to protect those lesser than him. It's a way to have your cake and eat it too (Heyman & Columbus, 2001).

Parents and kids can fall into this story pattern. The inheritance may not be for wizardry, but it could be anything, such as playing basketball, becoming a doctor, going to Yale, the possibilities are vast. The idea that the parents' "power" and essence is transferred to their children creates all kinds of potential conflicts. We have all seen the story of sons or daughters who want to follow a different career than their parents, to marry someone outside the family culture, or adopt a different religion. However, many times, the children do follow a path parents approve of and matches expectations for continuing on traditions. The children's heroic story matches the parents' story for the time being, but potential for deviation is always possible. This often creates a sense of unease, a feeling of anxiety within the relationship between parent and child. Many times this anxiety prompts parents to advocate for a particular path of family honor and heritage. This tactic may well work sometimes, but I have seen it also fail numerous times. It fails primarily because of people's drive to write their own stories, to feel in control of the world. Making a choice that's in stark contrast to other family members' wishes clearly shows that the hero is blazing a unique path that is all his own. In our examples of King Arthur, Luke Skywalker, and Harry Potter, each character pursues a family legacy that was hidden from them. Through their childhood, these characters are pushed by "normal" parental figures towards fulfilling a family obligation, but then as adolescents, the true family history is revealed. The new heritage is much more exciting than the standard family pattern, and it marks the character as special and separate.

It's commonly known that the best way to make teens dislike an activity is to push them into it. Yet for some reason many parents can't help themselves. They see the activity of inheritance as so vastly important that if only the children would experience and understand the rationale they will come around. Activities such as high grades, religious events, sports, or specialized training are important and highly desirable by many teens. But, when pushed on teens by their parents, interest in the activity is doomed. The hero has to eventually take on the quest willingly. With that said, the ideas of passing on power through family bloodlines is so ingrained in our stories it can be alluring. The best method to help children pursue their family legacy is letting them discover it on their own. Provide kids with opportunities to ask questions. Adults who quietly engage in legacy activities without making a show or lesson out of it invite curiosity. An adult might go one step farther and make it "secret" knowledge like Luke's connection to the force or Harry's history in the wizard world. Telling a child that they are too young to know the story or that they must earn the right has amazing power to invoke interest. Again, this is commonly known, but parents and adults too often get caught up in the story they have already worked out; that their child will take up the family mantle in a proud and effortless manner.

The final consideration of "passing down power" involves parents making a purposeful separation between their stories and their children's. In *Star Wars*, Darth Vader is searching for Luke Skywalker. We the audience think this is to destroy him in revenge for Luke's action in the first movie, but in reality Darth Vader has a different story in mind. He has created a narrative arc in which he is able to use his son as an extension of himself. Darth Vader will become more powerful and able to overthrow the emperor if Luke joins forces with him (Kurtz & Kershner, 1980).

When parents feel the child is a direct extension of themselves, as an outgrowth of the parents' power, the child can transform into surrogates of the parents (at least in the parents' eyes). In a lesser version of this, parents see the child as a representation of the family, as an example of the parents' skill in "parenting." There is an underlying belief that if a parent is good, the child will automatically act well. When the kid or teen begins acting in ways that go against this belief, such as "talking back" or tantruming, the parent feels not only frustration at the behavior, but also a strong sense of embarrassment. This embarrassment is what many parents struggle with the most. The idea that they are judged by the child's behaviors prompts them to take stern actions to curtail the kids, which of course invokes additional conflict. Further problematic behavior ensues, then more embarrassment is piled on, and the cycle feeds itself to a crescendo of rage. If adults continuously remind themselves that the child is not an extension of themselves, that passing on the torch of the family is different for each member, they can address the problematic behavior effectively without being emotionally triggered themselves.

8
THE BIG BAD

As stated in previous chapters, every story must have an antagonist, a villain. The villain represents the "other," the "enemy," the "out-group." There are many ways to demonize a character, but as we have also discussed, villains are most interesting when they are relatable, when they are the shadow of the protagonist. The villain who is just one side step from the hero's point of view is often the most menacing. For example, Luke Skywalker sees the path that he could go down when he is offered an alliance by his father Darth Vader. He could embrace "the Dark Side" and be just like his father. But what about Darth Vader's boss, the Galactic Emperor? This character is only mentioned in the first movie, seen in distorted holograms in the second movie, and finally makes his debut in the third movie. He is the "Big Bad," the unknown villain who we don't know the secret history of, the villain who represents "pure evil" (Kaminski, 2008).

The idea of inherent evil or goodness is seen in countless stories throughout time from all over the world. For example, the Judeo-Christian tradition has the Serpent, Lucifer, the Devil, while other cultural traditions favor the multi-faceted villain, such as in Hindu traditions where Kali the Destroyer is actually a version of Krishna. These two approaches to "evil" can be seen in most stories, where one, the other, or both exist. In many narratives, the villain is doing the wrong thing for the right reason and can be transformed by the acts of the hero and turned into an ally who will help confront the main villain, the evil incarnate villain, the "Big Bad."

The question of inherent goodness or evilness is a philosophical/theological discussion outside the scope of this book. However, what's critical for us is to know how these concepts play out in the stories of our lives. Is the villain in your story a Darth Vader who is twisted in his thinking by the tragic circumstances of his life, or the Galactic Emperor Palpatine who is "pure evil" and cares for no one?

As discussed in the last chapter, the idea of inherent metaphysical energy (vitalism) is the basis for most initial stories. In this perspective, a totally evil villain is the norm. This is because neurologically people use a mental rule of thumb (heuristic) of categorizing objects in the world as "good" and helpful to survival, or "bad" and dangerous to survival. The complex "shades of grey" that comes with understanding a villain's motive is part of an autobiographical story created in higher levels of brain functioning. Most children's stories begin by defining one thing (or person) as "bad" and another thing as "good". Nuanced and complex additions to the story come later and require practice. However, even when the simplistic good/bad dichotomy is rejected for more complexity, the groundwork is still there to slip into the basic story formula (the Dark Side is easier, faster, more seductive).

When children or teens relay aspects of their current story arc, the villain of the moment is generally painted as the basic "evil" villain whose sole purpose is making their lives miserable. This may be a teacher, a coach, a peer, or a sibling. As people get older and the brain further develops, it becomes easier to see people in our lives as shadow villains whom we oppose but also understand. Then, the basic all-evil villains are moved up a level as we create stories about people we don't have direct contact with, such as politicians, corporate leaders, or celebrities. Some people find the total evil story cropping up with whole groups that are considered "other," such as different ethnicities, religions, or nationalities. Interestingly, when people who advocate that a certain group is inherently "bad" are challenged to get to know a specific person (known to be "good") within the target group, there is usually a slight story change. The people acknowledge that the counterexample is "good" or "okay" but just an "outlier" and they still consider the group as whole to be "bad."

As parents and adults working with children, keeping these facts in consideration when intervening in their problems can make things much easier. For example, two young children are playing with toy cars and trucks. Let's name them Tom and Larry. They both want to use the same sports car toy at the same time. Tom is just a little bit quicker than Larry and he snatches the toy just as Larry reaches forward. The fact that Larry will get angry with Tom is not surprising. What does surprise some parents and adults is the way Larry voices his anger: "I hate him," "He's stupid," "He never lets me have the car." Adults know that none of these things are true, so why is Larry saying them? Little Larry's mind has suddenly cast Tom as a villain, a basic villain, an all-evil villain. This is normal, and with practice Larry will be able to see past the initial emotional pull and let his more sophisticated story stay dominant. For that to happen, he has to practice the skills of favoring other mental shortcuts and rules of thumb, perhaps "Sometimes friends fight" or "I can't always get what I want." These heuristics develop faster or slower in each child. Adults can remember this and keep themselves from going to the same mental place, "Larry is full of hate," "He's just mean." These thoughts come easily to mind and can become the dominant story if they are left unchecked, even in adults.

The fact that both types of villains exist in a story is also played out with kids and teens (and adults). In general, as people grow they are more and more able to keep the immediate villains of their story as flawed shadows capable of redemption. However, when emotionally triggered, this capacity is diminished and the old "all evil" mentality resurfaces. It's not uncommon for anyone to make these kind of declarations when highly upset.

In comic books, these ideas are forever being played out as heroes try to stop the villains they face, but not become villains themselves. Characters like the Punisher and Daredevil provide examinations of the two ways heroes possess potential villainy. The Punisher has embraced an "evil must be punished" mentality, and so anyone he deems as "evil" will be executed. This simplistic categorizing makes sense in many ways, but through the Punisher's stories, we see him constantly battling to apply his philosophy when the situation becomes more complex. The hero Daredevil faces the same challenges but he has taken an oath not to kill, to see the more complex picture. Yet, he finds himself engaging in the "He is all evil" mindset when things get really tough, such as when he is enraged at the actions of the villain. He must consciously choose not to cross the line into simple vengeance (Williams, 2016; Whitbrook, 2015).

Whether or not a person is in our "group" can be an indicator of how our mind will initially classify a type of villain. I have participated in many parent meetings about a "bad" teen's actions against a "good" teen. The "good" teen was of course the child of the parent in the room. Both parents were able to accept that their teen's actions were not always completely innocent, but the negative behaviors were quickly rationalized and the teen would become that sympathetic type of villain that could easily learn the error of his ways to make a full change. The "other" teen was characterized as inherently evil, whose actions were unforgivable and deserving of the harshest punishments. If both parents were in a room, competing narratives would bounce back and forth, much like lawyers in a courtroom. I had to remember that both parents believed their teen was the flawed victim, while the other teen was all evil. In our minds, the actions by someone in our group are easily justified but actions from the other group are the result of innate flaws.

The story we create to make sense of the world produces a filter for new information. As new events take place, as new characters are introduced, they must be placed into the current story. Once there, the characters are unlikely to change unless they inhabit a character archetype that involves transformation. If a person is deemed a shadow villain that has potential for transformation, new actions by that person will be seen as either staying on the dark side or making steps toward the light. Actions that they take in a positive and friendly direction are interpreted as hope and potential of the transformation. Alternatively, many parents may feel great frustration, anger, or dread around their child whose behavior is considered "bad," but the parent can remember that the child is a shadow version of themselves, making mistakes similar to their own youthful mistakes or similar to some other beloved family member. This creates a feeling that the child can change, that the villain will be transformed into an ally.

Conversely, if a person or child is seen as the evil incarnate villain, then any behaviors that person makes will be seen as either evil, neutral, or only as superficially good (actually manipulative). I have worked with many adults who have come to see certain children in this way. Sometimes, even parents fall victim to this way of thinking, not by choice, but because their unconscious story fell into the pattern. Once the character type is locked in, it's difficult to change. A child seen as "just bad" has nowhere to go in the story except to play the "heavy" in all situations. A key to spotting when a child is being cast in this way is if they are frequently accused of manipulation, first suspected of wrongdoing when there is an unknown perpetrator, or dismissed out of hand when offering explanations. Of course, all sorts of manipulation and inappropriate behaviors might actually be going on, and it's important to be aware of that. However, if a child is constantly and circumstantially being accused and demeaned as "bad," this is a sign that the child is cast as the "purely evil" villain, as the Galactic Emperor, as Voldemort, or as Sauron. Nothing the child does will be able to change that perception. The change must be made in the mind of the adult.

Awareness becomes the greatest tool in dealing with a situation where a person is cast as an ultimate evil. The problems only come if the initial emotional impulses are followed without question. Humans have the marvelous capacity to notice the story as it plays out, to use metacognitive skills (thinking about thinking) to prevent the subconscious story from taking total control. This is a skill that must be practiced and honed over time. Mindfulness meditation practice is one method to deliberately develop this ability, but really it's just a matter of developing a habit of double-checking a thought against a baseline. The baseline is a deliberately accepted value or belief. For example, if I have decided that "All children want to succeed," then I can check to see if my automatic thought that a child "just wants attention" is true or whether a different story is going on. Perhaps, there is something amiss that requires adult support.

Children and teens on the autism spectrum have an especially difficult time with this as their metacognitive skills may be inhibited. I have worked with many teens who have the capacity to see how they cast other people but they must be led to this discovery through carefully laying out specific bread crumbs.

> **Adult:** "Do you think that teacher wants to see you punished?"
>
> **Teen:** "Yes, he's a jerk."
>
> **Adult:** "He's a jerk because he wants his class to be quiet?"
>
> **Teen:** "He's jerk because he just is."
>
> **Adult:** "Okay, tell me more about when he's being a jerk."
>
> **Teen:** "Last week, he gave me detention."
>
> **Adult:** "Oh, he punished you for no reason, huh?"
>
> **Teen:** "Yes, I didn't do anything."
>
> **Adult:** "Do you think your teacher would agree? What would he say if he were here?"
>
> **Teen:** "He'd make something up, like I was being disruptive, but it's not true, it was Tommy that was starting it..."

This method centers on shining a light on the mental process going on, so the child can finally see it and understand how it's impacting his thinking and actions. It should be noted that as emotional agitation increases, the more difficult it can be to use meta-cognitive skills, and the more the tendency to fall back on the reigning "total evil villain" story increases.

Children and teens (and adults) will often bring up a string of negative behaviors performed by the "villain" they are squaring off with. In the moment, they are angry with the target and this creates a filter in which only thoughts that feed the anger will make it through. Bringing up counterpoints to these negatives will be simply rejected or rationalized away. It can be pointless to engage with anyone in a heightened emotional state if the goal is to bring awareness to the story being played out. My tried and true method for working with teens in throws of a tirade about someone or something else is to validate them. Again, validation is not the same as agreeing with them. People can be validated that their ideas and position are real to them, that in their story everything they're feeling makes sense to them. If I'm watching *Star Wars* and told that Darth Vader is the bad guy, then I can agree that makes sense (from a certain point of view). I can also mentally note to later describe to them the alternative story that shows him as a tragic lost hero.

On the other hand, our stories can cast a person as all good, as a "saint" who can do no wrong. It's the cliché parents who refuse to acknowledge their "precious angel" can do anything negative. Harry Potter's cousin, Dudly, and Cinderella's wicked stepsisters are just a couple of examples where adults dote over a child and see all actions as justified. These characters' existence in all types of stories is pervasive and as old as human civilization. Children and teens might experience a version of this phenomenon, often called "hero worship," glorifying adults or peers so that they can do no wrong because they are so good at one particular thing. These people may be professional sports players, actors, or celebrities. The "popular" peers at school might also fall into this category. Obviously, both versions of this type of categorization can be problematic.

Many movies and stories have been created to highlight how idealized individuals are not as all-good as we might think. In reality, all people have flaws and thus there are no "all good" people. An individual's flaws and negative behavior can be emphasized to pull a person down from a pedestal just as only focusing on positive attributes puts the person on the pedestal in the first place. Thinking that all of a person's behaviors are positive is as dangerous as believing that all are negative. Again, validation and fostering awareness is the most powerful method of using these story elements as a growth opportunity. For example, many people dislike Superman for being a "perfect" hero with no flaws, he's a "goody two shoes" with no pathos to make him interesting. That can be true when looking at Superman as a main character, but using Superman as a plot device, as something for other characters to aspire to, is a popular way to use the Man of Steel. The story becomes, is Superman really worthy of our praise? Batman has been given a similar treatment over the years. He is often portrayed in the "bat god" mode where all his choices, actions, and ideas are the right ones. In these stories, he is always one step ahead of the villain. This seems like it would result in boring stories, but they are not because Batman is not the protagonist. He becomes "Athena" or "Horus," a god of mythical power, guiding the hero and providing inspiration or even salvation. In these stories, his sidekicks like Nightwing and Robin take center stage and, in many scenes, they question Batman's decisions and actions. Should they really follow his lead? Will he always be right? In both the case of Superman and Batman, questioning the hero worship creates an interesting story to explore. In the end, there is of course nothing wrong with having an idol to look up to, the point is not to take it too seriously (Tye, 2013; Weldon, 2017).

The all-good or all-bad character is likely to pop up in our story at some point. It might be a child, a teen, a peer, a boss, or even the President of the United States. This character type is there because of our basic hardwiring of categorization. But, remembering that our minds are also capable of analyzing the story as it plays out gives us a unique ability to purposefully mold our story in new directions.

9
SCIENCE FICTION

In science fiction stories, current knowledge about the world is extrapolated to what the future might be like. The first story in this genre was Mary Shelley's *Frankenstein,* originally written in 1818. It is the tale of a medical doctor who discovers, through scientific investigation, the secret of life. He learns how to create the animating force that separates living tissue from dead flesh (Shelley & Rieger, 1982). In many ways, however, the novel *Frankenstein* is in essence the story of a son who feels rejected by his father and takes revenge. It's the story of a father wrestling with how to deal with his offspring whom he believes has descended into evil. The story could be told with "magic" instead of science, and, in the novel itself, the secret method of Dr. Frankenstein was never revealed. It wasn't until the famous movies of Boris Karloff that lightning and chemicals were used as the method of regeneration (Laemmle & Whale, 1931). Other films have used different visuals, like electric eels (Hart, Coppola & Branagh, 1994). On the surface, it might appear that science fiction simply involves adding technological trappings in place of a magician. However, what makes science fiction stories special is exploring how new knowledge effects society at large. How will personal stories develop when new technologies and discoveries are fully implemented?

The crisis in *Frankenstein* comes from the doctor's decision not to replicate his work, not to give his creation a bride. He makes a moral decision based on the future implications of his technology. This is what ultimately sets the two characters towards destruction. How to use knowledge wisely and recognizing that disasters can come from unhindered use of new knowledge is a key element of science fiction. This is why Mary Shelley's story struck a chord in the 19th century and continues to today. Applying new knowledge has been debated by scientists, philosophers, and theologians throughout history. This debate occurred before the term "science" was coined and comes in all shapes and sizes. It's for this reason that the foundations of sci-fi stories are so compelling: "What if doctors could resurrect the dead?" "What if advanced aliens came to Earth?" "What if a person can be genetically engineered?" The question of "What if..." is fascinating, it's another neurologically hardwired aspect of the human mind. We constantly make predictions based on current knowledge. We extrapolate to the future looking for potential resources and dangers. This process is constant and can't be stopped (Novella, 2015).

In the movie *Alien*, a group of "space truckers" are on their way home to Earth in a massive ship carrying tons of precious raw materials. They are awakened early from their cryogenic sleep because an alien spacecraft has been discovered on a planet they are passing. The space travelers are instructed by the boss corporation to investigate this discovery. It could be something extraordinarily valuable, something so new and unique that it's priceless. They do indeed discover an alien spaceship in which they find the remains of technology they don't understand. They also find pods carrying an alien organism. This alien grows into a terrible monster covered in slime, with massive claws, extending fangs, and acid for blood. It's a nightmare creature that slowly picks off the crew. In the end, it is defeated only after a revelation that the crew were betrayed by the company, that they were test subjects and sacrificed in the name of the new discovery (Hill, Giler, Carroll & Scott, 1979).

This science fiction story is one that many people see playing out in their personal hero's journey, not with an alien monster per se, but with something new and seemingly innocuous that leads to terrible danger and destruction. The fact that faceless corporations or governments endorse something only heightens the dread and tension in the narrative of many people. Again, the fear of the unknown and the new is hardwired into our underlying subconscious processes. Some call this the "status quo bias" but it's something that has been known for a long time. It's evident in the old saying, "The devil you know is better than the devil you don't." Meaning that, in general, people are willing to accept negative aspects of the current "thing" because the new thing might be even more terrible. The promise of improvement is not enough to overcome this thinking. The new thing is categorized as potentially dangerous and the "What if..." mind goes into gear. Our story can take a sci-fi twist in which new technology is viewed as a potential villain in itself. When something inevitability goes wrong in our lives, when something bad does happen, the cause is checked against potential dangers. New technology is an easy target. If we can create a plausible story to cast the new discovery as an alien monster, it will happen. All this goes on under the surface and outside of our conscious awareness. We just "know" that the technology is bad, the reasons come later. Mary Shelley introduced the western world to this style of narrative with her fears of medical science. It continues today.

However, as we noted, *Frankenstein* is not only about the negative consequences of technology, it's also an indictment of abandoning a child who needs guidance. This second theme is an extremely old story with nothing new to fear, but the first layer of "technology fear" makes it appear to be a wholly new type of narrative. In our modern life, overlapping these two themes makes it easy to blame science and technology for problems that have always been with us. This is because the appeal of demonizing new things feels better than the alternative of knowing that some problems keep coming back no matter what.

"Science" can feel like a villainous character but in reality it's a process. It's the specific process of making informed conjectures and then testing those hypotheses to determine the truth. This is common knowledge and taught in all elementary science classes. However, the part that's hard to swallow involves the impact on our personal stories. In the process of science, an individual's senses and personal narratives cannot be trusted. This means that one person's account is not necessarily considered objectively "true." It's one version of the event formed into one possible story. To illustrate this, consider the many movies "based on true events." The topics may be identical but depending on the filmmaker, every aspect of the story can be altered to create a particular villain, message, or emotion.

In the process of science, there are too many possible variables to give any weight to one observer, to one story. Random chance is the most critical to account for (Mlodinow, 2009). Consider a man on television claiming to have magic powers. He will demonstrate these powers by influencing the home audience's flip of a coin. There are millions of home viewers who take out a coin. The magician says he will make it come up heads. All the people flip the coin, and as randomness would predict, around half get heads. The viewers who flipped tails give up on the magician and change the channel, while the ones with heads stay tuned in but aren't convinced yet. The magician says "heads" will come up again. Everyone flips their coin. Again, half of the audience is lost when tails appears on their coin and switch stations, but the other half is growing more convinced. The process continues three more times, each time the number of audience members whose coin lands heads is cut in half. But in the end, the audience whose coin flips heads five times in a row still numbers in the thousands. These people are amazed, from their limited perspective it seems like the magician has real power. In reality they are self-selecting as "believers."

The mission of science is to uncover the truth of a phenomenon and ensure that what's happening is due to a specific identified cause, not simply the cause being advocated. This requires immense time and energy to collect lots of data from multiple viewpoints. This is cold mathematical data that many people don't understand. It's a far more compelling story when it's from a single point of view, not when several mathematical percentages are compared against each. In math, the narrative is actually sucked out and we're left with the pure abstraction of numbers.

As parents and adults taking care of kids, our job is to see how science works at this fundamental level so we can introduce new technologies into our stories in productive ways. We must keep awareness of the tendency to demonize the "new" thing as an "alien monster," a danger. Of course, at the same time, many "new" technologies that make great promises can be types of dangers, especially for wallets. The story of a new thing, especially a product for sale, is impacted by "marketing." This is a process of describing something in a way that fits into your personal story so that you either want it, love it, hate it, etc. The basic idea is to purposefully manipulate your narrative so that someone else benefits. This may be for noble reasons or it may be to make profits.

Generally, when it comes to scientific discoveries, there are two opposing pitches. The first, "Better life through science" is the science of *Doc Savage*, *Tom Swift*, and *Johnny Quest*. Doc Savage is the Man of Bronze, who masters a myriad of scientific disciplines and travels the world to thwart all manner of strange threats. The other view is the "mad scientist", the "evil professor" as with Lex Luthor, T.O. Morrow, and Professor Ivo. Lex Luthor was originally a classic maniacal mad scientist who spends time in a lab whipping up deadly methods for thwarting Superman. However, he has also been the suave billionaire inventor who uses his vast resources and intellect to create ultimate weapons of destruction (Tye, 2013).

Both of these approaches can work into someone's story because they create the character of "science" as a force for good or bad. Science becomes the ally or the enemy. In reality, "science" is simply a process of discovering facts about the natural world and "technology" is applying those discoveries in useful ways. Any message that tries to demonize or glorify this process is subject to scrutiny. For example, the "appeal to antiquity" tactic is used to glorify something "ancient" as better than something new. This makes inherent sense when combined with our fear of the new. Today, all manner of vitalistic medicines are advocated for that have no possible impact on health from a medical science point of view. They are remnants of ancient beliefs similar to Phrenology, the study of head bumps to chart personality types, or the four humors, a belief that four different bodily fluids cause all types of illness when they are imbalanced. Many vitalistic traditions advocated for pre-date germ theory and rely on the placebo effect. Yet, these products and services continue to sell because their narrative is so compelling, "Ancient secrets are far better than the new technology" (Novella, 2010).

The other side of the coin may propose that "science" has a magic solution. For example, every so often a new version of the perpetual motion machine is marketed to investors. The name might change to something like "quantum accelerator" (the word quantum is a popular way to make something sound like science). However, at the core, it will center on the idea of creating a device in which more energy leaves the system than enters it. This is of course impossible. However, many are tricked into believing it's possible because the story that's created about the machine is so compelling. The story usually involves a group of rogue scientists fighting the establishment to create a breakthrough. All they need now are investors to finish the prototype, but beware, the evil energy corporations are out to get them, so be cautious of naysayers. This story has been made into a movie many times because it's so compelling. Unfortunately, with perpetual motion, it will only ever be a story, yet the con usually works if it's dressed up in enough science jargon.

So, how should we view "science" when working with children and teens? Again, the key is maintaining awareness of how science is being cast in your story and the child's story. Is "science" a great ally and mentor or is it a villain and monster? If either is the case, then the reality is being missed because it is neither bad nor good. We tend to think in terms of only "bad" or "good" because our minds rebel against non-categorization. Without categories, the characters cannot develop and the story cannot progress. One method is to break down the idea of science into the smaller parts and see it as a process of many pieces. Any concept that is a character in our story can be dealt with the same way. Complexity is revealed the more one examines a concept and the more holding them in simple narrative terms gets harder. This process can also be applied to people, examining the details of another's actions, statements, and communications will break down the simple roles they are cast in.

In practical terms, becoming a savvy consumer of science can be as complex as you want to make it. Each area of study has expertise on even smaller areas, ad infinitum. Finding a reliable source for science information to guide your family can be tricky since many outlets will be selling the good science angel or the bad science devil.

When hearing about a new scientific discovery, fear, or technology, the first thing is to check for "face validity." Does this make basic sense? If not, then the burden of proof is on the one making the announcement. When an argument is made, anecdotal evidence or testimonials are worthless. As we discussed earlier, these people with positive results could simply be the ones who were lucky enough to get good results, just like the five "head" coin flips in a row. They genuinely believe in the thing but only because they don't have a full picture. Reading original research studies can be a great source of information but they are complicated and full of jargon. Finding a "meta analysis" is a good way to look at the overall view of a highly researched topic, but again these can be extremely technical.

Another method of analyzing a new scientific product or method is finding a laymen source of information that is known for its non-bias approach. How do you know if it's non-bias? First, ask "Do articles focus on the actual study that's going on?" and "Does it give prevalence to the majority scientific opinion?" This means, if 90% of researchers are in agreement, then 90% of the article is discussing this position, with 10% offering the much smaller held position. Unfortunately, most articles about science and technology fall back on classic journalism, giving equal portions of the article to each point of view. This works in most non-science subjects, but with science it makes it seem like a quack concept is on equal footing in the research community as that of a sound idea. This can result in all types of unneeded worry. For this reason, sources like Scientific American which specializes in science reporting can be a good reference.

The federal government is also a great place to gather information. The National Institute of Health runs a free database of research studies called Pubmed.org. The Center for Disease Control has loads of vetted information and the Food and Drug Administration validates food and drug claims. Also, when making most parenting decisions, it can be best to look to the local experts in your life. For medical decisions, contact a licensed physician. For educational issues, talk with trusted teachers, etc. However, just because a state licensing board exists, that doesn't mean the service has scientific validity.

Science, like many abstract ideas that have become characters in our stories, can be blamed for all sorts of problems that routinely crop up in our hero's journey. The story of *Alien* is in essence the story of finding a new strange land with unidentified scary dangers. This story is similar to the Incas and Aztecs who encountered strange men wearing metal armor, carrying weapons that exploded like thunder, and riding giant alien creatures (Diamond, 1997). These invaders began killing and conquering in ways that seemed just as unthinkable as an acid blooded xenomorph tearing his way through a spaceship. The stories remain the same. This is not to dismiss the impact of technology on culture, but this impact usually alters the genre of the story, not the plot.

Remembering this fact can keep focus on values, beliefs and expectations at the core of conflicts. When the printing press was created, many railed against unleashing the floodgates of knowledge. Did the printing press cause conflict in the world? Absolutely, but it wasn't the machine that printed letters on a page, it was the belief that knowledge should not be secret, that everyone can interpret sacred writing. A person may disagree with the idea but it's not the machine that's bad, rather the machine forces us to reexamine the issue. The spreading of information has only expanded over the centuries. Radio was demonized as a waste of time and dangerous to the young. Comic books were called a scourge of youth, while television was denounced as making people less intelligent. Today, video games were accused of reducing attention and social media is accused of increasing conflict. All these bad guys of technology are really new versions of the same problem. Should some knowledge be kept secret? How do I make young people meet their obligations? How do I stop children from fighting? These questions were written about in the ancient stories, are written about today, and will be written about in the future. These questions are the plot of the story, the underlying conflict that must exist for the story to exist.

So as adults working with children and teens, we can model how to best play out these story lines. We can highlight the old conflicts and dramas that are being brought to the forefront when new discoveries and technologies are impacting our daily lives. We can share with young people the solutions of the past and how they can continue to find new solutions in the future. We can avoid the trap of demonizing or deifying new technologies. Avoiding the cliché, "Back when I was kid..." seems easy at first glance, but in reality the fear of newness creeps in constantly. It requires awareness and vigilance to avoid turning whatever's new into Frankenstein's monster. It requires lifelong learning to not be swayed by doomsayers who advocate the new "scourge of the young." It means staying informed about the complex problems of life that most likely require complex solutions.

In our modern society, many fears have been brought up around information technologies. Much has been made of problems of connectivity in cyberspace. Again, these are old problems that don't need any special kind of attention beyond the problem-solving that is happening around the specific issues. Helping kids be aware of other people and of making safe choices will always be a concern, only the details of the methods and protocols will vary as people connect in new and different ways.

10

A SCI FI PROBLEM

In many of our personal epic stories, science fiction elements sneak in even if we don't recognize it. As we saw in the previous chapter, looking to the future is inevitable and applying recent discoveries about the natural world to our current story is an automatic process. Categorizing is what the mind does, constantly creating labels for sensory experiences, creating "things". These mental constructs, "things", are then put in larger mental "boxes" in which they seem to best match. The matching process is not always perfect. Our mind might note that 3 of 4 critical attributes match, so it goes in a certain mental category. But what happens when only 2 out of 4 match? Sometimes, the mental object is attached to an old concept (box), while sometimes a new category is created, perhaps even a sub category. This is often referred to in psychology as assimilation versus accommodation. We even create categories for the ideas of making categories (Damasio, 2010; Novella, 2015).

With this in mind, let's examine another "old" problem that has been given a new "scientific" conceptualization. Today, it's often called "genetics" (the colloquial, not technical meaning), but it's also been known as "eugenics" and "nobility." In reality, it's the old problem of categorizing people and then making judgements about those categories. Sadly this old problem interferes with actual advances in understanding how biological forces affect the stories of children, teens, and adults.

Most of us know the story of Hercules (or Heracles, the Greek version of the name). In this ancient tale, the king of the gods Zeus fell in love with a mortal woman and they had a son named Hercules. He was half god and possessed powers beyond other men and women, especially super strength. His divine bloodline set him apart and made him both the target of supernatural enemies and able to become a great hero/king (Cartwright, 2012). Stories of Hercules and other half gods have been passed down over the millennia from cultures all over the world. From ancient Mesopotamia came the epic story of Gilgamesh, the demigod King (Mark, 2010). While other parts of the world have offered their versions. In the history of China, Persia, Egypt, and the Americas, rulers have claimed either divine birth or to be a god in human form. Great monuments and religious orders grew around the worship of these people whose special heritage set them apart from the rest of the world and entitled them to rule others. Entire groups of people have claimed dominance over other groups due to the belief that the progenitor of their group was of divine or supernatural origin (Garland, 2015).

Of course, if one group is elevated, then other groups are denigrated. For example, beliefs that some groups are inheritors of ancient curses due to their progenitors' crimes which results in the belief that those groups deserve to be treated harshly, to be conquered, to be exploited. Ancient stories play out this plot line over and over, either at the level of entire societies or at the level of single individuals. At the core, these beliefs purport that people inherit strengths and weaknesses from their ancestors and thus their values can be determined by examining their ancestral groups.

In modern society, we call this story element "genetics". Consider the *X-men*, a comic book created in 1963 by writer Stan Lee and artist Jack Kirby. In this story, certain humans are born as "mutants", which are people with special powers. These powers are the result of the individual's inheritance. The powers were dormant or non-existent in their parents. The mutants' genetics were transformed so that they could do amazing feats. This origin was expanded over the years by various writers who explored how these characters would be viewed by society. In most versions, the X-men are hated and feared because they are different and potentially dangerous. The leader of the group, Professor X, runs a school to train mutants to use their powers for the good of society. He is contrasted by Magneto who forms the Brotherhood of Mutants, a group that wishes to use their powers to conquer. The Brotherhood maintains that their powers demonstrate they have evolved beyond normal humans, giving them the right to rule. Many analogies to the civil rights movement are weaved throughout the X-men stories, such as national protest against them, a movement to make mutants register with the government, and the fact that Magneto was a survivor of the Jewish concentration camps of Nazi Germany (Hiatt, 2014).

In the time of Nazi Germany, the story of human ancestral inheritance and the right to rule was forefront. However, the Nazi regime was just one of numerous groups who advocated a version of the old idea of inheritance called "eugenics." In this framework, it was believed that humans improved over time as each individual was "bred" with others who had the same superior qualities. This was thought to result in whole groups who were genetically superior. Eugenics was a theory most directly created by Francis Galton who was heavily influenced by Darwin's theories of natural selection. Galton devoted a great deal of energy to discovering how certain human traits were passed down in offspring (Bashford & Levine, 2012).

It is widely known that animal and plant husbandry can be used to create new and more desirable versions of an organism. Modern horses, dogs, and corn are the results of "genetic engineering," which is purposefully breeding idealized traits into offspring. Applying this concept to humans wasn't groundbreaking, but the eugenics movement sought to understand the details of the process and exploit that knowledge. Not surprisingly, by using this framework, political groups found new reasons to believe they were superior to others and new justification for why their tribe should rule. No longer was it because of divine ancestry but evolutionary superiority that was en vogue. However, the story arc remained the same - finding a reason why our group is "better" than your group (Bashford & Levine, 2012).

Notwithstanding the importance of the science of genetics and the many great insights gleaned by the early pioneers of the field, those pioneers often could not separate their research and philosophy from their own personal heroic journey. They fell victim to the "old story" - the story where the righteous people take divine retribution on the evil hordes of inferior people. In the early 20th century when eugenics was growing in popularity, many writers incorporated the ideas into epic science fiction stories.

One writer, Frank Herbert, created a futuristic fantasy universe where a feudal system of planetary nobility rule over various space systems. (The concept of nobility itself goes back to a belief that God had ordained certain families to rule.) The stories in Herbert's universe are known as "Dune." In *Dune*, a group called the Bene Gesserit has been working for over ten thousand years to interbreed individual nobility in order to create a superman, a messiah figure. This comes to pass in the hero of the story, a young nobleman named Paul whose family is killed and his holdings are taken by a rival noble house (Herbert, 1965). What sets the story of *Dune* apart is the intricate descriptions and analysis of what a culmination of genetic breeding might look like. However, the failing of the *Dune* eugenics and all eugenics as a science is a reliance on what is called "Lamarckism."

Lamarckism was a rival theory of species development in which a parent animal can develop a capacity over time and then pass this trait onto its offspring, who then in turn continues the progress. The classic example of this disproven theory is that giraffes have long necks because in each generation the animal pulled and strained to get the higher leaves, so the development of those neck muscles and structures were passed down to offspring. In this view, the efforts of the parents towards honing a specific trait is not only advantageous to the parent, but to all subsequent generations (Bashford & Levine 2012). In *Dune*, each member of the breeding program can access collective genetic memories to possess vast unheard-of knowledge. Later in the *Dune* saga, genetic clones are created and their genetic memories awakened to create identical copies of characters whose body and mind can be resurrected countless times (Herbert, 1981). The idea of passing on established knowledge and skills makes inherent sense and this idea has been passed down in stories from antiquity. Often, a child is seen as the continuation of the parents' story, taking on the parents' quest and representing the family through time. A father who is known for skill with a sword is expected to have a son who is also a master swordsman. In today's world, it's common for parents to attribute a child's love of sports, or cars, or cooking, to a parent's interest in the same subject. However, the parents do not believe such love of the topic was "taught" to the child but that the skill is inherited from a parent's own great skill.

As many people know, the basic idea of Lamarckism is considered false and scientists generally accept that an organism's traits are inherited through parents' genetic material. New traits are the result of random mutations being selected as beneficial for survival. In Darwin's view, the only criteria of being beneficial is if the parents survive to pass on the trait. While many people disagree with this idea due to theological objections, the truth of how organisms' traits are created from a big picture view is beyond our current scope. How our personal stories make sense of traits that are inherited by children from parents is the important part for our discussion.

The classic tendency is to reaffirm the belief that our group, our tribe is the best, and we'll use whatever plot device will support that story. Again, this process is not consciously chosen, it just happens as a default unless there is awareness of the process itself or some other story supersedes it. All of this is complicated by discoveries in genetics that have great implication in helping parents and children. Doctors can now test for a variety of diseases before a child is born and prepare interventions right away. In my work as an educator and psychotherapist, the topic of autism has been a primary focus that often centers on the idea of "genetics." Autism has changed in scope and definition over the years. Currently, the Diagnostic and Statistical Manual (2013) uses the term "Autism Spectrum Disorder" and describes the behaviors required to be formally diagnosed.

However, the behaviors described in this version of autism are known to many parents who may or may not consider their child autistic. As with many psychiatric conditions, the disorder is conceptualized as a spectrum where all people display the behaviors listed at some point and in some degree, even if it's minimal. A disorder is noted once the target behaviors meet a threshold of frequency, but a great variability still exists. Many people who meet the formal diagnosis of autism are able to function well in most aspects of life. These "high functioning" individuals formerly had a separate diagnosis called Asperger's Syndrome which has been removed from the DSM-V.

Traits labeled as "autistic" have been observed in many people through history. For example, the idea of the socially awkward nerd who loves to talk about one or two things and has difficulty with new situations. The character is a standard trope in many stories. In the 1985 action adventure film *The Goonies*, we are brought the standard version of the character in a boy named Data who loved technology and inventions. He provided the team with gadget resources throughout the story of teens seeking an old pirate treasure through a labyrinth of traps (Bernhard & Donner, 1985). Data was part of the peer group and accepted, but his role was limited.

Other "nerd" characters in stories aren't so lucky or they too are only accepted in a comic relief or utility manner. Another 1985 science fiction adventure, *Explorers,* showed how "nerd" characters might be given more range and cast as a hero. *Explorers* told the story of three boys who were given knowledge of alien technology and used it to build a spaceship to meet the alien space travelers in person (Bombyk, Feldman & Dante, 1985). The two lead characters embody certain types of nerd characters but there is also complexity in them. As written in the script, the characters in *Explorers* could have been basic tropes and nothing special but for the performance of the actors, Ethan Hawke and River Phoenix, who brought an underlying emotionality to the roles beyond what was written. This understanding and conveying of subtle emotional signals is a fundamental capacity and skill that most kids labeled as autistic struggle with.

A child who meets autism criteria can seem detached, uninterested, and robotic. It's often not as simple as what's being said or done, it's all the intricate subtlety of communication. This can create great difficulties in schools where social hierarchies are most stringent. Young kids play out their heroic stories and kids who seem even a little different are given sharply contrasting roles. Kids who meet autism criteria often have difficulties beyond "not fitting in," they can be depressed and frustrated since their desire for friendship and understanding is no different than a typical child.

Parents who watch kids struggling are often desperate for a solution. Giving a medical name to the situation can be helpful but it can also be misleading. As with many mental disorders, there is no underlying pathogen with autism, nor is there any biochemical test to validate the condition. The word "autism" is simply a way to describe a set of behaviors that many people display and which cause difficulty in their lives. Adults can grasp at all kinds of straws in trying to find the cause of the condition, which implies a "cure" to follow. Autism is a condition that verifies the impact of genetics on children. While eugenics and breeding superior humans is thoroughly discredited, the other extreme view of humans being a blank slate in which only experience matters is equally not real.

The genetic inheritance of each person gives a baseline. The story can unfold in infinite directions from the base, but it's still a major factor. A boy whose parents are both six foot five inches tall has a higher probability of being taller than his same age peers as he progresses through childhood. The genetic cause is not mysterious if both parents have tallness as a common attribute in their family history. The boy may be ostracized and taunted for being different or he may be admired for extreme prowess at sports. The story can take many twists and turns as the boy uses his genetic inheritance in his own heroic journey. With autism, the same circumstances are in play, but "tallness" is not generally considered a disease. An inherited trait that is advantageous is usually handled easily by kids and parents. Traits that can lead to pain or suffering are another matter.

The parent of a child labeled autistic can begin to fall back on the old Lamarckian mindset, that something they did in their lives caused the condition. This story casts the parent as a villain. It's a way to make sense of the situation that feels compelling (even if it creates self-loathing). The bend toward Lamarckian explanations is similar to looking towards curses and conspiracies. A villain needs to be created, it may be inwardly directed or outwardly. I've heard many versions of this story with parents blaming all manner of things for their child's autism from fluoride water to astronomical objects. Invariably, in my personal experience, the mental drive to create a story prompts a parent (usually the mother) to lament her choices in life as causal forces in her child's story while the other parent (usually the father) displays behaviors that match the child's, a clear indication of genetic inheritance. A mother sitting in front of me may be genuinely distraught and proclaim a strong desire to know the cause of her child's autism, and I can't help thinking, "Have you met your husband?"

The reason why the genetic connection is not obvious is that adults have often developed coping skills and methods to compensate for inherited qualities. For example, I may not like to look someone in the eye, it might be painful, but with practice and gradual desensitization training, I can do it regularly because I understand the importance in social greetings. Another person might not have to devote any energy to meeting someone else's gaze, to them it's natural, perhaps even pleasurable. In the end, we both get the job done and can be successful. When adults meet and get married, they only meet the refined version, the man or woman who has practiced to cope with difficulties. The child is born with the raw traits and none of the parent's efforts to cope with the underlying genetic inheritance. Unfortunately, the child must find his own way to cope. The parent who did not struggle with symptoms of autism sees only that something is wrong, something needs to be fixed.

With genetics, we all inherit advantages and disadvantages, traits that can be helpful, neutral, or painful. As technology and medical science continues to advance, our society will be able to use genetic information to understand and influence people in new ways. Someday, there may be means to change genetic traits instead of simply coping with them after the fact. Many sci-fi stories have examined this idea from various angles. Will genetically engineered super soldiers attempt to take over the world as in *Star Trek: Wrath of Kahn*? Will genetic engineering lead to a new type of segregation as with the film *Gattaca*? As we noted in the last chapter, with science fiction concepts, the problem itself is an old one. In the end, it comes down to dealing with the villain. Autism and other conditions can become the archenemy and central to the story or they can be assimilated as another dimension of the character. For me, it helps to keep in mind that all people have attributes that can be strengths or weakness depending on the context.

11

FORESHADOWING

In the opening credits of *Back to the Future*, a single shot takes the audience on a tour of Doctor Brown's clock collection and contraptions. In filmmaking terms, this shot lasts a long time. Most shots last less than 5 seconds, and if shots last a long time, the content of those frames should be extremely interesting. In *Back to the Future*, the long continuous shot works because the strange devices of Doc Brown's morning routine keep our attention. We love these gadgets that make breakfast in strange and overly complex ways, but what the audience might not notice is all the information about what is to come communicated through these objects (Canton, Gale & Zemeckis, 1985).

The obvious informative elements shown in the above mentioned long shot include a framed newspaper clipping describing how Doc Brown was formerly rich but that his mansion burned down resulting in tough times as well as framed pictures of famous inventors like Thomas Edison and Benjamin Franklin. The radio is clicked on by a device declaring the month and year in a car commercial, October 1985. The TV clicks on and a news report explains that plutonium was thought to be missing from a power plant. A dog food can is opened by a robot arm, adding to the pile of food not eaten on the floor, showing no one has been home. The more subtle clues of the future are the clock decorated with a "bum" drinking under a street light and a man hanging precariously from the long hand of a miniature clock tower. The last of the shot shows us a skateboard that rolls across the room to knock into a radiation-proof bright yellow storage chest (Canton, Gale & Zemeckis, 1985).

All of these elements will come to play in the movie as we watch. Doc Brown, with his trusty dog Einstein, has made a last effort to be a successful inventor by creating a time machine powered by stolen plutonium. Marty must eventually duel the villain of the film and he wins through clever use of a skateboard. The year and date play a central role as the two characters struggle to power the time machine by an elaborate setup, much like the breakfast machines. In the frenzy to make the setup work, Doc Brown hangs from the real clock tower moments before it will be struck by lightning. Finally, we know when our main character Marty McFly makes it to his home era because of a homeless man sitting on a park bench, much like the man on the clock (Canton, Gale & Zemeckis, 1985).

The classic descriptor for this aspect of storytelling is "foreshadowing" which is the act of showing or telling an audience about the future of the story in subtle ways. It's the act of establishing the "causes" for the story's dramatic twists and turns. These causes may not seem obvious at first and, in fact, the best stories make foreshadowing a subtle act that operates below the radar. As we watch a movie or hear a story, we might not know how something is important, but we know it is important in some way. An old screenwriting rule known as "Chekhov's gun" says that if the audience sees a gun loaded in the first act, then they must see the gun fired in the third act. In a movie, everything has the potential to be meaningful and reappear in the end to make a huge impact. In fact, it's expected. If the author can provide clear foreshadowing elements and yet trick the audience into not noticing the connection until the end, the emotional impact is all the more powerful. The opposite is also true. If we see a gun loaded at the beginning of the movie and never see it again, we feel that something isn't right. Conversely, if a gun is suddenly drawn that was never established at the beginning of the movie, something is equally amiss.

As we discussed in previous chapters, the human mind is a prediction machine, constantly craving connections. A story's requirement to include foreshadowing illustrates this need in a condensed format. When the world is connected and those connections suddenly make sense, we feel a sense of catharsis, a rush of emotions, relief, and energy. This feeling provides us a baseline for moving forward, if we feel confident in understanding the connections between cause and effect, we can take actions with reasonable certainty about the outcomes. In movies and stories that people create, everything is connected. If the main character bumps into someone at the coffee shop, it might turn out to be the new boss at the company. The character that was wronged ten years ago turns out to be the key to solving the new mystery. The object found at the beginning of the story provides a vital clue of how to succeed against the villain. Almost every movie and story plays with this symmetry.

In the opening of *Back to the Future*, we are given a glimpse into the McFly family. They are struggling, obnoxious, and tragic. The hero of the story, Marty, seems to be the only member aware of the problems that exist. The father is exploited by his boss, works a menial job, and seeks escape to the past through old TV shows. The mother is out of shape, drinks heavily, is cantankerous, and yearns for old days. Marty's older brother and sister seem stuck in dead-end jobs. At the dinner scene establishing these facts, Marty's mother just happens to speak of how the parents became a couple and the circumstances of that night. This information forms the basis for Marty's interventions in the past as he attempts to recreate the situation after unintentionally disturbing it. At the conclusion of the film, we're given a similar family gathering scene except, thanks to Marty's interventions, the family is now markedly improved. The father is a successful writer while his rival and former boss now cleans cars. Marty's mother no longer looks out of shape and seems positive about the present. Marty's brother and sister have high-end jobs (Canton, Gale & Zemeckis, 1985). This symmetry of before and after an intervention is ingrained in our thinking. We can't tell progress unless it's compared to something else, ideally the same subject in the past.

The human mind's thirst for cause and effect, for foreshadowing elements, and for symmetry has aided people throughout history. However, it also creates a myriad of false positives, situations where a connection is believed, but does not actually exist. People can't help but look for foreshadowing signs of what the future will be. In reality, we are constantly besieged by sensory information and then the mind creates filters for deciding what is important, what should be part of conscious attention. Unfortunately, the cause and effect machine has a habit of identifying a "cause" only after the effect has occurred (Novella, 2015; Mlodinow, 2009). For example, say an Asian man and a white woman rob a bank and then drive off in a purple sports car. An hour later, the police pull over a couple in a purple sports car matching the description. Even without evidence, the couple is arrested as the police reason, "What are the chances that a couple matching that description located in the vicinity of the crime are not the perpetrators?" On the surface, the chances seem low. There are several variables involved that seem to match, but without knowing how many other people in the area might also match the description, we cannot draw any probability. There might be in reality three couples in a ten mile radius who match the description making the probability one in three.

Thinking probabilistically is a definite limitation of human cognitive processing. We crave connection so much that actual probabilities rarely occur to us (Mlodinow, 2009). A famous example of this is called the Monty Hall problem, based on the game show *Lets Make a Deal* (Selvin, 1975). Imagine a contestant is told that behind one of three mystery doors is a new car. She must choose a door and if the car is behind it, it's hers. The contestant chooses a door. This is somewhat boring as it's just a matter of a one in three chance of getting the car. It's all random. But the host throws in a twist. Rather than opening the selected door, he opens one of the doors not chosen to reveal a bogus prize. Now two doors remain. The contestant is given the opportunity to switch, to change to the other closed door. Should she do it, does it matter? Most people would say it doesn't matter, it's still a one in two chance. But the truth is that the contestant should definitely change her answer, she will increase her chance of winning. To illustrate why, imagine the game consisted of 100 doors instead of three. The contestant chooses door number 1. The host then opens 98 other doors to reveal no car. Now, only the original chosen door and the door marked number "58" remain closed. Should the contestant change doors? Yes. Vital information was revealed in showing that none of the 98 doors held the car! What is special about door 58? Is it more likely that you chose correctly the first time or that the prize is behind the door that had to remain hidden by the host who knows the secret?

Parents and adults working with children often have an inherent drive to find connections. This need to identify foreshadowing can be pervasive. Parents often look to early childhood milestones like speaking or walking "early" as an indication of greatness to come. For example, a child "reads" their favorite picture book out loud. The parent is impressed because this book is "advanced" for the child's age. The parent then assigns a cause, like "My child is a genius," or "My child is a gifted reader." These types of explanations tend to be the most pervasive for many parents because these stories are compelling, they feel good, and they are exciting. The high reading ability foreshadows a life of advanced academics, perhaps as a super scientist like Doc Brown. A sense of pride can develop when the child is seen reading, because as we have noted, the child's story is often viewed as a continuation of the parent's story. In Western culture, we love to put numbers on these kinds of predictors. Perhaps the most famous in popular culture is the IQ test (Intelligence Quotient). In many movies, a quick and dirty way to establish a character's intelligence is to mention the character's IQ score. A parent might brag about a child's IQ score as an indicator of potential specialness over an entire lifetime.

What this kind of thinking misses is the many other causes that may be contributing to the observation of "Reading an advanced book." A book that has been read to a child many times will often be memorized, with the child "reading" the story using the pictures as a guide of what to say. Alternatively, a child who is reading with a parent will often rely on hints and prompts from the parent to get through a passage. As adults, we often can't help ourselves from doing this or even notice we're doing it. In research, this is called the "observer effect." When we make an observation of a system, there is a tendency to think we are outside of that system, and that the results we see would be there no matter what. In reality, by making the observation, we become part of the system and affect that system, it can't be helped. Today, experimenters take extreme measures to address this problem. For example, when a fast food company tests new products, a subject might sit in a stark white booth with no one around, a panel slides open, and food is just there. They eat the food and fill out an automated questionnaire (Ariely, 2010; Mlodinow, 2009).

Parents usually don't go to these lengths and will often influence their children's behaviors in tiny subtle ways that result in the foreshadowing we take so seriously. A parent with lots of books in the house, who often reads for pleasure, and makes it a daily ritual to read together with a child, will likely have a child who is "advanced" in reading. This is a real effect, and while the child's skills may actually be advanced for their age, this may or may not result in profound outcomes for the child over their entire life. They may be advanced in some way, at some point, but it's also likely that other children will catch up to make that difference much smaller.

All this is to say that our foreshadowing brain will create a story around observations about what the future will hold, and often this story will not play out the way we expect. Of course, this is not necessarily a bad thing. Some parents find the foreshadowing clues of their children's future to be ominous signs of disasters. Perhaps a young boy loves to play video games with guns and violence of all sorts. Does this mean he will grow up to be a violent criminal? No, not at all, at least no more likely than other kids. Parents will often look for these signs with the honorable intention of intervening early, but as we noted, so many false positives make appropriate interventions difficult. It can be difficult to take a probabilistic view when the stakes are high. After tragic shootings by teens, it was often pointed out that they loved violent video games. It makes sense to our storytelling mind that the video games created violence in the child, but this is a logical fallacy known as "post hoc, ergo propter hoc" (after this, therefore, because of this). We see two things in succession, the mind makes the connection that most matches the story we are telling, or emotionally want to tell (Mlodinow, 2009; Novella, 2015). If I want to demonize video games, then any opportunity to make that justification will be done in my mind all under the radar of conscious thought. In truth, if video games caused increased violence in youth and adults, then we would see an increased number of violent crimes as video games have proliferated society. However, in reality, violent crimes continue to decrease over time and have been decreasing for decades (Pinker, 2011).

One exercise to help combat this tendency is to purposefully create several alternative stories as to why an "effect" was observed. If a child is not completing homework, we might jump to "He's playing too many video games," because this is a behavior I as a parent don't like and I'm looking for justification of my position. It's helpful to stop and purposefully consider other stories, such as, "He's having a hard time doing boring tasks," "He doesn't have the skills needed for the assignments," or "He's depressed about being rejected by a girl." The possibilities are endless, yet we as adults will often latch onto one "cause," the one we noted much earlier as a possible bad omen. We chose to notice this detail because it pricked our sensibilities, it bothered us at an emotional level. However, this trick of the mind is the same as deciding that I'm "unlucky" and then justifying that position by noting all the negative events of the day. However, I can just as easily decide I'm "lucky" and justify it by noting all the positive events.

Of course, this doesn't mean to ignore all observations as many behaviors can actually be a sign of an underlying difficulty that can be addressed directly by adults. The key is keeping a purposefully open mind about the potential causes. The famous case of The Bell Curve illustrates how real effects can be carefully measured but easily attributed to dubious causes. In this study, researchers found real data that demonstrated differences in intelligence scores between social and ethnic groups. The data was not flawed in that no purposeful manipulation was done and the data was collected using established procedures. There was a real difference between groups, but deciding a "cause" was what made this study infamous. The authors made a case that an inherent difference in intelligence between social/ethnic groups was the cause in the data showing different measures of intelligence. However, many social scientists have since pointed out that tests of intelligence are based on reading skills, verbal English skills, and cultural awareness skills. Children who are not native English speakers, whose families live below the poverty line, and who are not part of the dominant western culture, will of course have difficulty on standard tests, but not necessarily because of a lack of intelligence (Herrnstein & Murray, 1996; Gould, 1994).

Regardless of the cause, the main point is that many children do not perform as well as others in schools and therefore interventions are needed. Finding the right intervention can often be a trial and error process, as various "causes" are considered. Perhaps children of poverty need additional resources provided by the school that children of higher socioeconomic status are provided privately at home. Perhaps there is a learning disability and the student requires alternative teaching strategies. Perhaps the child is suffering from acute environmental stressors such as violence in the home. Again, the possibilities are endless and complex. Adults must be patient and understand that many factors may be operating at once and that any one intervention may not be enough to overcome all factors.

The good news is that many "effects" that are a concern and should be examined will actually reduce significantly as the child grows. In many cases, the intervention is not about getting rid of a behavior but compensating for it to maintain daily functioning while natural maturation will improve behaviors over time. Unfortunately, many programs and treatments will report to "cure" people, when in reality the child was given support enough until his natural processes caught up.

All children are different and grow in different ways. If we look for signs of danger, we'll probably find them just as if we look for signs of greatness, we'll find those too. A great illustration of the power of expectations was a study conducted by Rosenthal & Jacobson, (1968) in which teachers were told that one group of students were expected to be more successful than another due to results of intelligence testing. In reality, the groups were randomly assigned. In the end, students identified as intellectually superior were indeed more successful. The teachers were observed to be holding the "gifted" students to a much higher standard and their instruction included numerous small extra interventions. This was not done on purpose but subconsciously as the teachers played out the stories that were foreshadowed for that group (higher intelligence means more success). Parents and adults who work with children cannot escape the power of foreshadowing but they can be aware of the effect. They can make purposeful effort to see the story that is being created and learn to look beyond it.

12

HEROES OF HORROR

A group of young twenty-somethings arrive at a cabin in the woods. It hasn't been used in quite some time, and they shouldn't be there. They just think it's a great opportunity to have a fun free weekend in the forest. If the owners happen to come by, they'll make up some excuse, like the car broke down. As the three couples get settled in, they notice the office is full of strange creepy objects including a book with an odd cover. This cover looks to be made of leather with a grotesque face carved into it. The book itself holds arcane writings on old dirty pages. When an audio recorder is turned on, we learn that the cabin belonged to an archeologist studying an ancient "evil" text. He of course does not believe in superstitions and records the translated words of the "Necronomicon." The young partiers are rattled, but brush it off until they are besieged by terrifying phenomenon. Each in turn is possessed by spirits, transforming into grotesque fiends who attack the others. The group is picked off one by one until a lone survivor is able to dispel the spirits by destroying the magical book. This is the story of *The Evil Dead* (and Evil Dead 2), a horror movie made for little money in 1981 by a young director named Sam Raimi (Tapert & Raimi, 1987).

In the decades following 1981, Sam Raimi has become an immensely successful and famous director, but his success is in many ways based on a cult following and fan fervor that grew around his horror movies. Horror movies are just one method of telling a certain kind of story, the ghost story or monster story. While science fiction is a relatively new genre, scary stories of the supernatural have been told since ancient times. Most cultures have beliefs and stories regarding the underworld or lands of the dead, but horror stories are something different. They are designed to illicit a sense of dread, fear, wonder, intrigue, and often terror.

Fear is a primary emotion triggered in the "oldest" parts of the human brain. The physical reaction to being scared has been widely studied and documented. Adrenaline surges to prepare us for a life or death struggle. Blood flows into the legs to prepare for rapid flight, sometimes this reaction makes people lightheaded enough to faint. The fear response is easy to trigger even when our conscious mind knows that the danger is not real. When Jason slashes a machete, Freddy Kruger slices with his bladed fingers, or Michael Myers slowly stalks forward, we feel that rush of adrenaline even though the images are clearly only projections on a screen. When we ride the roller coaster at a theme park, it's hard not to feel some kind of rush even though the risk of injury is no greater than driving in a car down the freeway (Damasio, 2010).

Horror movies and theme parks remain immensely popular. Halloween is a national holiday celebrating all things scary and magical, and it's a billion dollar industry. This situation is strangely paradoxical. If asked, "Would you like to feel intense fear?" most people would decline. Yet, many seek out this feeling as if it were fun and enjoyable. Parents often engage in the time honored discussion of "It's too scary for you," when a child wants to watch a certain movie or hear a certain scary story. Parents are worried about the aftereffects when the child can't go to sleep. This is a valid and logical concern. If children watch a scary movie, they may not be able to separate reality and fantasy enough to not be scared when alone in the dark. They might have nightmares of the story and awake in a state of panic. For me, the more interesting issue and question is, "Why does the child want to watch the horror movie in the first place?"

The answer to why we want to watch horror movies involves the different types of situations in which the scary story is experienced. How much fear is expected? How much control do we have over the story? Imagine sitting in a dark movie theater with ominous music blasting through massive speakers, we see the image of a girl walking slowly down a dark hallway lit only by candlelight. The view jumps to the inside of a room, a man in a strange mask stands hiding, the moonlight from the window glints off a massive blade he holds ready to strike. The candlelight illuminates the woman's approach, she slowly pushes open the door unaware that that the maniac is hidden just behind it. She slowly moves into the room raising the candle. Yellow light spills inside. We see the knife wielding arm raised to strike... This is when many people watching the movie will close their eyes, hide their face in their hands, or look away. Most people watching are scared for the woman. We are frightened for what will happen to her. The viewer feels a level of fear but they also have a sense of control. The film has made us an omni viewer, as we see the perspective of the woman as well as the killer. We know that the danger is there. The intensity comes from our concern for the woman, but we all know what is likely to happen. Some viewers will watch to see if the woman is struck, they can handle that kind of feeling, while others decide to look away as the feeling of fear is too much, so they must take a break from the story. In total, the viewer is in control of the situation even though real fear is coursing through them.

Now, imagine a different movie. The young woman moves slowly down a darkened corridor. The hall is old, dirty and covered in cobwebs. Rotting wallpaper and moldy wood floors denotes a house abandoned for many years. The woman holds a candle illuminating her face and only a few feet beyond her. Outside this zone of light is complete darkness. Ominous music plays as she walks slowly forward, and we only see her and her viewpoint of utter blackness beyond the candlelight. Anything might be there, ready to jump out. The music begins to swell, she passes a closed door. Suddenly... In this story, we the audience have a limited point of view. We know only what the character knows, along with the fact that it's a horror movie and something bad has to happen sometime. As the girl moves down the hallway and the music intensifies, the feeling of dread intensifies for most viewers. Some may hide their face at the beginning and peak through the gaps in their fingers every few seconds, others may look away entirely until it's over. Both know something will leap out (known in moviemaking as simply a "jump scare").

In the second movie scene, the foreknowledge is not the same as seeing the villain's position and understanding the entire situation. The feeling of fear grows gradually but steadily. Some viewers can't cope so they hide in their fingers or other covering as a method to sooth themselves, and once the fear goes down enough, they want to rejoin the story. A peek through the fingers helps filter the fear. Knowing that blocking the images is easily achieved by closing the finger gaps is soothing. If nothing happens, the fear again builds, prompting another full retreat into the hand shield. Most of us have done this, or at least seen others do it. It's all about controlling the level of fear. We want to have some feeling of fear as it's exciting when adrenaline rushes, the heart races, and other neurochemicals begin streaming. This can all be "fun." However, there is a point at which fear becomes "panic," when the conscious mind is no longer in the driver's seat and the primal brain takes over. For many, navigating this breaking point is part of the experience, part of the fun. How close to panic can I push myself? However, this is only the case if we possess good coping skills and strategies to reduce the fear as it grows towards overload. Reminding myself that it's only a movie and shielding my eyes can be a great tactic. Many people don't understand that fear is not a "thing" that is there or not there, it's an ever present feeling that grows or reduces in magnitude over time.

For children (and many adults), the idea of entering a potentially frightening situation can be alluring. The game of fear versus panic can be fun. But when they actually experience it, it becomes clear that the necessary coping skills aren't up to the task. Panic wins out. Many parents can relate anecdotes of their child wanting desperately to meet a costumed performer, but as they get close and interact, the interest turns to terror and the boy or girl bursts into tears. A classic example of this is sitting on Santa's lap, which was fantastically portrayed in *A Christmas Story* as the young protagonist Ralphie and his brother visit Santa at the mall. The brother can only scream in terror after being plopped onto Santa's lap. Ralphie is older and has some better coping skills but he is still "dumbstruck," not even remembering why he came in the first place (a typical fear response). We, the audience, see from the character's point of view as the standard mall Santa Clause appears maniacal and menacing (Dupont & Clark, 1983).

As our central premise dictates, we are the heroes of our story, a story that requires elements of danger and fear. Feeling threatened and endangered is part of that story, it's expected. Some people become despondent on the other extreme because they cannot find the right intensity of fear to make their story meaningful. They might turn to skydiving or driving race cars. In the story of *Fight Club*, a man becomes so desperate to feel excitement that he creates an underground fighting club, which escalates over time into an anarchistic terrorist group (Bell, Linson, & Fincher, 1999). Again, all these behaviors are attempts to control the story and find the right level of fear, not too much but not too little and in durations that are desired.

Panic invariably does come to most people at some point during a fearful encounter. Being placed in situations where fear escalates into panic and one's coping strategies are insufficient to handle the fear is something that everyone is vulnerable to, but some more than others. In general, children have less coping skills for fear, their threshold into panic comes quickly. They often have little idea of how to handle the feelings. Indeed, we all know that young children cry and tantrum over stressors that appear slight in magnitude. As children grow up, there is often an expectation by adults that children will naturally gain more coping skills, and that their threshold from fear to panic will increase without any direct interventions. In many cases, this is true. However, for numerous other children the capacity to work with fear, to prevent panic is something that they don't master even into adolescence. This could be due to physical neurological conditions or it could be due to a lack of cognitive skills, and is often both.

Conditions like Autism Spectrum Disorder often come with skill gaps related to emotional regulation. A child with ASD might have above average skills in memorization but lack skills in self-soothing. Mental skills, like physical skills, take practice. Memorizing facts is one such mental skill while self-soothing is a different mental skill. A child is more likely to practice skills that they find enjoyable such as batting practice for baseball lovers, drawing for aspiring artists, and memorizing facts about a beloved topic for others. In contrast, developing self-soothing skills is often painful and takes desensitization practice. Choosing to develop a non-preferred skill because of its advantage in the long term is hard for most people.

Our job as adults is to be aware of the difficulty entailed in developing a cognitive skill such as self-soothing and be willing to give instruction and encouragement in learning the new skill. For example, children learning self-soothing skills can be coached in deep breathing, active imagery, and self-affirmations.

Of course, recognizing the difference between real panic and "manipulations" can be difficult. A child may tantrum at the anticipation of a panic attack. Many adults struggle with this, where specific desirable situations are avoided for fear that a panic attack might come. A person may become irritated and upset when forced into these situations, not because of a full blown panic attack has occurred but because the fear of having a panic attack is ever increasing and the feeling of being out of control is growing towards the panic threshold. When we notice that fear is escalating but panic has not won, we know this is the time to aid the child (or adult) in using self-soothing strategies, to run through the tactics that can handle the upcoming feelings. For many of the children that I have worked with, letting them leave the room for brief breaks helps. The students were allowed to go by themselves into a separate room for a predetermined amount of time (it varied by student need). That amount of time was calculated to be just enough to keep them below the panic threshold but still be challenging and require self-soothing practice. I compare this to diving, in which the diver has to come up for air but can stay down longer and longer each time. Some teens tried to take advantage of this system, but I was always okay with that because it was my job as the adult to recognize this and intervene as needed. Expecting children and teens who lack critical cognitive skills to completely self-regulate is often not tenable.

For adults who have trouble recognizing the differences between real panic and manipulation, there are a few guidelines I found helpful. First, real panic is usually intense, the child simply flees and if they can't flee they attack. One of my students, an older teen girl, claimed to have phobia of insects. When a bug was seen, she screamed and yelled, but it was the scream of a "B-movie" actress, a "scream queen" performance. She didn't try to run away, she could have a normal conversation in between blustering statements about how scared she was. For her, the intervention was, "Feel free to step into the other room and come back when you're ready." There was no soothing words or "help" in calming down, because this is what she was controlling for, increased sympathy from others. At first, she refused to leave and elevated her screams and shouts. The other students were trained to ignore her and she was given the choice of leaving if the insect was too much or staying without disrupting class. Eventually the "panic" about insects went away as she found other more appropriate ways of gaining sympathy from others.

Contrast this with a student who panics at the sight of an insect and then gets up to leave. He reaches the door and is asked what's wrong. "The spider!" is all he can mutter. I say, "It's okay to go but you'll need to come in at lunch to make up the time." He might nod in agreement. The student returns a few minutes later and subtly asks, "Is it gone?" I reassure him it was removed, he comes back in and serves the time at lunch. He was genuinely willing to give up free time in exchange for fleeing from the source of panic. I think of this tactic as "price of admission." If a behavior is worth some kind of negative consequence, if its value is greater than something I know is extremely difficult for the child (like detention), then they've paid the price of admission.

For some people, they are thrust into situations where fear can suddenly escalate into panic and they have little to no control. This state of constant fear escalation on the brink of panic, or constantly fighting against the urge to panic, can create unique challenges. The symptoms that result from prolonged heightening of fear and panic is now labeled Post Traumatic Stress Disorder. In World War I, it was known as "shell shock," as soldiers fighting in horrendous conditions with massive casualties over extreme lengths of time developed symptoms in which the panic mechanisms of the mind short circuited. A person might become numb to most stimulus and then suddenly be hypersensitive to others. They might suddenly burst into a panic or rage due to a tiny stimulus, and yet have no reaction to other big events. Also, they might have intrusive thoughts and nightmares, waking up in a panic and even feel as if they they are reliving the high stress event (American Psychiatric Association, 2013).

The "Berserkers" as set forth in Nordic (Viking) oral history also closely match this phenomenon of "shell shock" or PTSD. In these tales, warriors who constantly battled in melee combat with axes, clubs and blades would suddenly seem to lose conscious control, attacking anything in a furious rage, both friend and foe. When not in combat, they seemed different from other warriors and civilians. They might be distant and then suddenly attack without warning over a trifle matter like losing at cards. Medieval stories hypothesize that these men became possessed by animal spirits that drove them to a frenzy in battle. From a certain point of view, this is accurate. The primitive mind takes over in times of panic and when the load on the cognitive system is too great for too long, an unpredictable burst of the primitive mind could result (Dunning, 2017). In modern society, soldiers, emergency responders, victims of abuse, and anyone in a "panic" situation are susceptible to developing these types of conditions. For those suffering from these symptoms, it's best to consult a licensed medical professional who can engage them in treatments that are shown to be effective. Generally, these include some type of cognitive and exposure therapy (U.S. Department of Veterans Affairs, 2017).

In the end, fear is ever present, a driving force in thought and behaviors. We embrace fear in many ways as it's an integral part of our stories, and we even seek out fear to get the rush that comes with it. A final consideration is preventing our children's stories from turning in the "horror" direction by keeping a wide perspective on what becomes the monster in our own stories. The human mind is good at identifying certain types of dangers: quick moving objects in our peripheral vision, rot and decomposition, as well as signs of disease. Other dangers can be harder to intuit. For example, many people will argue that society is more dangerous now than the past. Statements like "It's not like when I was kid" are often used to justify this position. However, in truth, the data clearly shows that violence worldwide is going down, and has been going down for centuries. Where does the perception come from that crime is on the rise and that society is more dangerous? Most argue that the main factor is the vast increase in media coverage (Pinker, 2011).

While crime rates have gone down, reports of crimes have skyrocketed, giving viewers a false impression that crime is high. This is due to a type of mental error called the "availability heuristic." Another way to think about it is the old saying, "To the man with a hammer, the whole world's a nail." We take the information available and subconsciously make assumptions that this is representative of all cases. A child who picks up a toy and gets a small cut on a jagged edge might then be careful picking up other toys, making the assumption that most toys will have dangers because the first toy did. As an adult, I know that the defective toy was a fluke and the others are perfectly safe, so I grab without worry. I have access to much more information because of my increased experiences. Yet, even as adults, we make this error frequently, and often create monsters in the process. If not careful, these monsters find their way into our children's stories (Novella, 2015).

An example from my own childhood is the infamous episode of the sitcom *Punky Brewster* entitled "Cherie Lifesaver." The episode was intended to teach kids about CPR, but it needed some conceit for the characters to use their CPR skills. The solution was to have Punky, the young girl main character, save her friend Cherie after being trapped inside an old refrigerator. For most of my childhood, I assumed that old abandoned refrigerators were a plague on society. It's not until adulthood that I could slay this evil fridge monster (Duclon & Dielhenn, 1986).

13

MONTAGE MIND

In the classic movie *Rocky*, an unranked boxer named Rocky Balboa is given a shot at the heavyweight championship title as a publicity stunt. The current champion, Apollo Creed, can't find an opponent willing to fight in a July fourth weekend that was already booked and promoted. The fighters who could actually challenge Creed would need more time to train and prepare. The solution is to offer the title bout to an unknown fighter who hasn't got a real chance anyway. The unknown boxer will agree to fight just for the publicity and Creed won't lose all the money he has wrapped up in the event. Everybody wins, or so Creed thinks, except that Rocky is going to give Creed an actual challenge. Through the film, Rocky changes from a mediocre fighter to a real challenger. The audience knows this for sure at the end of the famous montage when Rocky resolutely finishes a running session by bounding up a long series of stairs. Once at the top, he dances about, shadow boxing, and finally shoots both fists triumphantly into the air. We believe he's ready to face the challenge (Chartoff, Winkler & Avildsen, 1976).

Is Rocky really a challenger? What did we actually see? The sequence included 22 shots of Rocky exercising that lasted 2 min and 43 seconds. The shots jumped between running, pushups, and boxing practice (sometimes with sides of beef). These activities seem fairly standard when simply listed out. We have no idea how long he ran, how fast he ran, how many pushups he did, or if hitting sides of beef is an effective method of boxing training. On close inspection, it would seem that any boxer or just any person in decent physical condition could easily replicate this montage as it's just 3 activities that culminate in about 3 minutes of activity. Of course, we are to believe that this is a representative sample, a glimpse of many countless hours of training, yet that message is never spelled out. Our mind quickly fills in the gaps and we find ourselves believing that an immense amount of work has been expelled by the character (Chartoff, Winkler, & Avildsen, 1976).

The power of the montage is in the quick shots of progression, jumping between activities intercutting the beginning, middle, and end of each one. There is no need for dialogue because music provides the means for merging all the shots together. This is the same technique used in music videos. All the unnecessary elements are removed and we are left with pure simple story plus emotionality provided by a song or music. In the case of Rocky, the powerful music became the hallmark of the franchise and a standard for montage training scenes ever since.

Why is it so easy for us to believe that Rocky is now ready to fight after only a short series of exercise clips? The montage technique is a version of what our brains do naturally. As the mental story of our lives is being created, we note and incorporate elements that add to the story, that make it more interesting, that move the story forward. Any bits that don't seem important are not included. If I inquired, "I'd very much like to know what you did today, please tell me about it thoroughly, be specific, and don't leave anything out." The respondent might say, "I woke up around 7:30, had a shower and got ready. I ate breakfast and then went to work. I finished a presentation and met a friend for lunch...." This most likely sounds familiar. In reality, listing every action in a day would take more than the day itself. Describing actions like, "I stepped out of bed, raised my arm to the clock, clicked off the alarm, lowered my arm, went into the bathroom, gazed in the mirror..." would be endless. Each of these tiny actions are generally not added to our story because our subconscious has deemed them unimportant to the overall narrative (Novella, 2015; Damasio, 2010).

To improve a skill, it generally involves doing the activity over and over again. Tiny improvements are made over time, but these changes are so slight they are difficult to notice from day to day. As the skill is practiced, it feels like a repeat of the previous day, as well as the day before that. Only by using some kind of external measure can we truly understand the growth. By taking snapshots of the beginning, middle, and end of training, our mind can appreciate the progress. Essentially, we create montages in our own mental stories as a means to see our own growth and it just feels right - the same way montages in movies feel right.

Without developing this mental montage, it can feel like no progress has been made and even experts may see their skill as nothing special. They haven't emotionally internalized their progress towards expertise because the mind skips over the "boring" parts of a story. For example, daily practice that is only slightly different than the day before is not registered as exciting and ends up on the cutting room floor unless effort is made to chart the progress. This phenomenon is why many experts are terrible teachers as they don't really know "how" they do what they do, they just do it. Many children have had that certain math teacher who expects students to just "get it" like they do. When asked to further explain the math concept, the teacher simply repeats what was already said in the main lesson. This is where the expertise of a special education teacher is valuable even though they may not be an "expert" in the content area. They can approach instruction of "content" from many different directions and in all sizes and shapes.

A more pervasive problem created by our montage mind is acknowledging the amount of effort and practice that long-term goals require. A great example of this occurred regularly in my time working with teens labeled as autistic. Each year, with some slight variations, a student would request that the class do a special project, such as "build a robot." While there were many reasons this probably could not be accomplished, my response was to not shoot them down outright, but see it as a learning opportunity. The request generally seemed to be something the teen was passionate about, so I wanted to be encouraging. However, the lesson to learn was not about building a robot, but about how to break down big goals into smaller tasks. I would agree to consider the project as long as the student was willing to do the work required. They would eagerly agree to this condition. An initial task was to find a resource to use, so the student was asked to locate a handful of websites that could provide instructions. Some students dropped off at this first step, but many did manage to locate articles and websites about building a robot (or whatever special project they were interested in). After selecting a site or article that I knew was within their ability to decode and understand, the student was instructed to read the article and create a list of steps or tasks. At some point, the teen ran into something that was unknown, a concept or skill. I would show them how to look up this unknown knowledge and volunteer to help with specific difficulties. No student made it past this stage unless I pushed them, making the project an "assignment," offering extra credit, etc. Even with incentives, the necessary background knowledge of related skills and knowledge would grow and most students could complete something interesting, but usually not what they had envisioned to begin with.

This is a situation where teens have a strong desire to learn a skill and produce a product. They have whatever resources they need and an adult willing to aid when roadblocks are hit. Yet, few of my special education students proceeded past the initial steps without external pressure to continue. This is not the case for many "typical" teens. Most kids and teens can devote the time to master the small steps needed to reach the long-term goal; to develop the related skills and knowledge that complex projects require. For them, the daily practice of these skills becomes just another unimportant task that blurs into the next day, like brushing teeth. Their montage mind can summarize progress but also appreciates the daily practice in the moment, or at least tolerate the tedious practice tasks. Many teens and children I have worked with who have significant problems at school seem to lack this skill that I call "boredom tolerance."

My "robot project" teens could see a montage of progress in their minds viewing snapshots of tasks that leapfrogged from novice, to craftsman, to expert in a short time. However, the problem arose when they attempted to tackle many of the tasks required in a complex long-term goal like building a robot. They would run into to a situation where the knowledge or skill required was not interesting. Learning how basic circuits work or repeating tedious movements of construction tasks requires using the mental desire to obtain the long-term result in order to overcome resistance to completion of boring tasks. A child who desperately wants to play a certain song on the guitar might practice scales for hours knowing that it's a step towards the goal. Other kids lack the "boredom tolerance" and without aid they can only engage in tasks that have obvious interest in the moment. Indeed, my students would often become experts in drawing a specific character or reciting facts about a specific video game. They enjoyed the initial task, drawing the picture or reading about their favorite video game character, so they repeated it. They continued to repeat the preferred task over and over, improving their skill and knowledge in this tiny niche subject.

The key to understanding why these special education students can become "experts" in a certain specific area but remain unable to master their required schoolwork is the pleasure they get from one and not the other. Adults would often argue that if a boy can memorize all the statistics of a video game then he can remember his times tables. The short answer is yes, he is capable; but memorizing times tables is boring compared to video game factoids. The skill he lacks is "boredom tolerance." When confronted with boring goals, the montage mind assumes a 1, 2, 3 and done framework. Children or teens might want to succeed and after being given a great pep talk by caring adults, they seem ready to do it. However, in the children's minds they see the montage, the quick path to success. Adults will sometimes feed into this thinking with statements like, "It's not so hard," or "It'll be over before you know it." The children are then excited to begin because the montage mind is telling them it will be over soon just like when Rocky became a great boxer in less than 3 minutes. When reality hits and the feeling of boredom kicks in, the montage is shattered and the children can't continue. Many adults have also experienced this. Watching commercials for exercise and diet programs engage the montage mind, setting us up for feeling excited to begin the 1, 2, 3 and done process. However, as the truth sets in that losing excess body fat is a slow laborious process, many drop out of the programs.

Overcoming and avoiding the feeling of boredom is a central activity of a person's life, yet it's often not addressed directly. The storytelling mind edits our experience to create the hardwired narrative structure. Beyond just the montage, every story is an abridged version of events. The editing of a movie creates the story just as much as the writers, directors, and actors. Everything is shrunk down to the most interesting and important aspects. For example, if a scene begins with a man entering a room, the shot actually begins with the door halfway open as the man is already stepping inside. If a scene ends with a man leaving a room, we seem him turn towards the door and the shot is over. The viewer doesn't need the beginning or ending because it's filled in automatically. When the "edges" are not trimmed off, the movie feels slow and tedious.

This need to get to the good stuff, the important stuff, is another hardwired aspect of human biology. In the ancient "cave man" world, staying still was not a good idea. Finding the recourse to survive was an ever present struggle. Those who were idle and didn't focus on the objects of interest like food, water, etc., didn't make it. Humans have a survival urge to pursue the unique, the interesting, and the important (Brooks, 2012). Our heroic stories center on these elements. Focusing on seemingly non-critical tasks just feels wrong, it feels dangerous. So, by default there is a strange uncomfortableness when just being still - an "itch" that is usually not analyzed beyond "I'm bored." We feel it and learn to cope, but we also alleviate the discomfort whenever possible.

For many children, teens, and adults, the skill to deal with boredom effectively is never developed, so dysfunctional strategies are used instead. Some kids learn to cause chaos wherever they go, as a method to keep things interesting. Some will grab and investigate any object around them searching for new experiences. Teens will use their cell phones (mini computers) to access all manner of interactive and interesting content like social media or video games. Adults can sometimes try to alleviate boredom through food, TV binge watching, video games, and even illicit drugs. Again, this compulsion to get rid of boredom is considered typical of babies and toddlers, but as kids grow it's assumed that their ability to tolerate boredom will improve. For most kids, it does without much effort; however, for some it is much more difficult because this skill to tolerate boredom did not develop at a "normal" rate. Whatever the reason, these kids, teens, and adults can benefit from direct training in dealing with feelings of boredom.

One technique that has pervaded the world of psychology in recent decades is Mindfulness Meditation. This practice comes in various colors and flavors but is based on the idea of diverting conscious attention to mental activity and physical sensations in the present moment. The practice involves staying physically still and focusing on a present moment anchor, traditionally this is the breath. In this state, the "observing mind" or the internal watcher (storyteller) can begin to develop awareness of the separate feelings and thoughts that bubble up and fade over time. There is a tendency to get caught up in these thoughts and feelings. Resisting this tendency is a skill and, just like any skill, it takes a great deal of practice to become proficient. Getting lost in thoughts and feelings can be insidious. I may think "Breath in, breath out, breath in, breath out, okay, I'm focusing, this is easy, I wonder how much longer I should go..." That's all it takes to get lost in thought and pulled from the here-and-now breath. Focusing on breathing will bring up the feelings of boredom that push the mind towards any kind of interesting activity (Siegel, 2011).

If we've made a commitment to being physically still, then internal activity can alleviate the boredom. Our mind can wander in planning, storytelling, memories, etc. This is the primary method for many people to deal with boredom. A child sitting in the classroom is supposed to be quiet, look forward at the teacher, and listen to a rambling lecture about plants, the battle of New Orleans, the Pythagorean Theorem, or some other random piece of academia. This is boring and the feeling grows more intense over time, but the child will be punished for moving. The solution is to sit still, look forward, but not necessarily listen. He thinks, "I can remember my video game from last night and strategize about tonight's play." Usually, this is not noticed and the teacher seems satisfied with the student. Most of us have made it through a boring event by daydreaming. Mindfulness meditation is a step beyond this type of stop-gap strategy. The goal is to fully experience "boredom," to analyze it, sit with it in the moment, similar to placing attention on an itch but not scratching it. Doing this builds a kind of mental separation between thoughts, feelings, and the "thinker." It builds a capacity to handle feelings of boredom directly and has been shown to help in all manner of difficulties (Siegel, 2011).

However, mindfulness meditation takes a certain amount of dedication. This requires an awareness that a problem exists. Many adults can do this, but often children and teens cannot. Kids and adolescents see no problem with avoiding boredom at all costs. Some don't understand why adults can't just leave them alone with their video games, phone or whatever. Often, teens in my class would lament that school was boring and I should make it "fun."

In light of the "boredom" problem, I worked for many years perfecting a program to maximize the natural interactional tendencies of children. My program was unique in my school in that it gave teens choice and access in what they learned and how they learned. In the end, while I could clearly demonstrate growth on all academic, social, and emotional goals, I decided to shut down the program because my school formalized a position that our priority was not to offer innovative education to our special needs students, but instead to prepare them to succeed in public schools. This necessitated a complete shift in focus, from harnessing a human's natural tendencies, to teaching teens the skills necessary to function in an environment designed to be difficult. Public schools were originally designed to provide basic instruction for all people in reading, arithmetic, and citizenship. Going beyond these basics was not required, graduating from high school was an accomplishment. Many people did not graduate and that was fine as they would become farmers, laborers, or factory workers where they learned skills on the job. Of course, the world has moved on and a high school degree is now the lowest of basic requirements, yet still necessitates knowledge in obscure academia that was originally meant only for gentry who had time to kill on superfluous pursuits (Gatto, 2001).

To be successful in public school (and many other environments in the modern world), one must acquire the specific cognitive skill of being able to tolerate boredom - having a high "boredom tolerance." I've found good results in making this an overt goal. In some cases, children and teens are given goals like "do homework," but this misses the point. For many children and teens, the work is not the issue, it's the "home" part. They go home and have access to all sorts of great ways to entertain themselves. Purposefully engaging in a laborious and boring task is overwhelming. For these children, adults can help by making the practice about dealing with the boredom. Kids will want to make it about the actual task with questions like "Why do I have to learn this?" My response was, "Finish the assignment and we can talk about it all you like." It's also helpful to give children specific strategies to work with difficult feelings of frustration when besieged by boredom, such as taking mini breaks, having a clean work station, or doing work right away after school. However, in most cases I've been involved in, building boredom tolerance with homework and other tasks means acting like a personal trainer. This means standing over the student and alternating between encouragement, directives, and validation. Every moment of doing homework can be like lifting heavy weights, each second is agony. The mind expects 1, 2, 3 and done. If it's not done in the montage time, then the long-term goal or immediate threat must be enough to overcome the feelings of boredom. For kids and adults, it's about purposefully developing the cognitive skill to handle this situation in ways that work. Helping children and teens through this is also a long tedious process and therefore the adult's sense of boredom also kicks in. A child is given an intervention and 1, 2, 3 it works, right? No, that's the montage mind telling you that "fixing" the homework problem will be easy and done in less than 3 minutes. In truth, it takes hours and hours of standing over a child giving seemingly endless directions. Years later the progress will be obvious and it will be safe to make a montage.

14

DEUS EX LEVIATHAN

In the film *Army of Darkness*, our hero Ash is possessed by an evil entity. It literally enters his body and emerges by creating an extra eyeball on the shoulder. This grows into a second head and finally Ash splits into two full-sized people. The two men look identical, but the copy is clearly not like our hero Ash. When questioned about his identity, the doppelgänger explains, "I'm bad Ash, you're good Ash, you're goody little two shoes." Evil Ash begins to mock and dance repeating "goodie little two shoes." Suddenly, hero Ash levels a double-barreled shotgun point blank against the evil twin's face. Blam! Evil Ash is launched twenty feet away with the mighty blast. Hero Ash steps triumphantly forward and remarks, "Good...Bad...I'm the guy with the gun." Leading up to this current film, the character Ash had been through a lot as he had already survived two movies of battling grotesque ghouls, ghosts, and monsters. Now, he's trapped in the past on a quest to get a magic book and he's just sick of the whole thing. He simply wants to go home and be done with the mess so he's going to assert himself by force. It doesn't matter if it's against something "evil" or "good," if it's in his way, it's pushed aside (Tapert & Raimi, 1992).

Many stories involve the use of force. The hero and villain may both use the same methods of violence with the only separation being the targets of that violence. In the opening scene of *Star Wars*, stormtroopers are killed as well as rebels, but we see the faces of the killed rebels while the troopers lay in white armor, more like robots than people. In later *Star Wars* movies, the heroes slay antagonists who are actual robots, while the bad guys kill biological aliens (Kurtz & Lucas, 1977). Sometimes, the hero may employ violence but only just enough and doesn't cross the line that villains do. For example, Batman will fight criminals, punch them, threaten them, and injure them in all kinds of ways. But this is not due to anger, it's calculated. He may pretend to be angry but just enough to provoke the villain in the way he desires and of course he will never use a gun or kill anyone, at least in the comics (Weldon, 2017).

As we examined in previous chapters, our stories are built around achieving goals and those goals are blocked by "our" villains. To reach our objective, the villains must be dealt with. The simplest method of doing this is pushing them out of the way. Violence is part of our world at every level of life, including microbes, plants, animals, and people. Stories of violence can be found in our most ancient text and the oldest of oral histories. The creation story of many cultures involves the fight between supernatural beings. Many are familiar with the ancient Greek myth of Zeus who kills his father to assume reign over the world. Zeus was not thought to be evil or wrong, he was worshiped as the rightful ruler of the sky. All this is summed up in the old saying, "Might makes right" (Pinker, 2011).

Sometimes, all it takes is the threat of force. In *The Princess Bride,* the hero Wesley lays in bed, weak and drained of strength. He has snuck into the evil lord's castle to rescue the princess, but the only problem is he can barely stand. At full strength, he was unmatched in swordsmanship, acrobatics, and unarmed combat. His reputation is well known. Now, as he lays on the bed, this reputation is all he has. The evil lord barges in to challenge Wesley to a duel to the death. Wesley accepts but offers strange alternative stakes. In place of a duel to the death, Wesley proposes a duel to the "pain." Of course, the lord is confused. Wesley goes on to describe with specific detail the horrific mutilations that he plans to inflict on the noble. Shaken by these descriptions and Wesley's reputation, the lord is primed to surrender. All it takes is for Wesley to stand, raise his blade, and dramatically demand that the lord give up, which of course he does. This bluff was just as effective as actually fighting (Scheinman & Reiner, 1987).

Indeed, threats can be just as pervasive in our stories as actual violence. They can win the goal without actually expending the resources of a fight. The trick is whether the villain and enemy believe the threat is real. The philosopher Thomas Hobbes proposed that violence is the result of one of three scenarios. The first two are fairly simple. In the first one, the enemy has a resource that is desired so they are attacked, and the resource is taken. As to the second one, the enemy is believed to be an imminent threat (an attack might occur at any moment), so the defender takes the offense and attacks first. Even if they don't win, there is still an advantage in that now the enemy is weakened so the anticipated attack will not likely take place (Hobbes & Macpherson, 2003; Pinker, 2011).

The third scenario is more complex. A group is unlikely to be attacked if the enemy believes that the price to get a resource is too high in that the struggle will be so costly that the prize is not worth it. This requires a reputation that the group is so strong that that attacking is not worth it, but this begs the question, "How to create this belief without actually engaging in all-out attacks?" The answer is to use any small slight as an excuse to establish this reputation. This creates the idea of "honor" fighting. For example, suppose a man is called a coward at a party, he draws his sword and challenges the insulting party to a duel. The gentleman who made the offending comment does not think a casual insult is worth potential injury so he retracts his statement. Now everyone knows the price of making an insult and imagines the price of a bigger offense. It's easy to imagine this scenario in any setting, bikers in a bar, gangsters on the street, or children on the playground. These three types of violence, including defending of honor, are engrained in our stories (Hobbes & Macpherson, 2003; Pinker, 2011).

What can keep these patterns of violence in check? What can keep violence from escalating all the time? The ancient solution was total annihilation of an enemy tribe. If no enemy is left, then they can never retaliate or become a threat again. This occurred often in the ancient world; the Romans supposedly sowed salt in the fields of Carthage to ensure that nothing could be grown again. In 1651, Thomas Hobbes, came up with a solution he called, the "Leviathan" (Hobbes & Macpherson, 2003). The Leviathan is a metaphor for an external authority (also known as government) wh ich has the strength to impose peace on everyone. However, in any story the Leviathan can change in scale and take many forms (Pinker, 2011). In ancient Greek plays, the Leviathan was an immense force in which a god would descend at the end of the story to stop the conflict and sort everything out. In screenwriting, this is called *"deus ex machina"* (god from the machine) and it's considered a big problem for a story. If a movie ends in this fashion, it feels unsatisfying as there was no winner, no payoff for all the hardships the characters faced. We inherently know a victory must be earned and if something outside the story suddenly swoops in to save the day, it's cheating (McKee, 1997).

Adults working with children and teens will often find themselves in the position of being both the enemy and the Leviathan. When working with children, the goal is often changing their behavior, doing chores, completing homework, staying quiet, going to bed, etc.

These are clear parameters, but in many ways the issue of "honor" is overlaid on this conflict. Again, this notion of honor is another subconscious aspect of how we create stories to make sense of the world. We feel that if honor is threatened then we are vulnerable to future attacks. Thus, defending honor means ensuring safety and victory in the future. This is a feeling that occurs before and outside conscious thoughts about an incident (Damasio, 2010).

In *A Christmas Story,* when the young protagonist Ralphie attacks the school bully and repeatedly strikes him we feel a sense of relief, of justification, of satisfaction. Thoughts such as, "He deserved it" occur to us. But did he? The instigating incident occurred when the bully threw a snowball striking Ralphie, it was quite fluffy and no injury occurred. He then mocks and taunts Ralphie for crying. The bully is using attacks against Ralphie's honor, not physical attacks. Many children are taught to "walk away" in these situations. Yet, in the film we have Ralphie's point of view. We feel his anger at being dishonored and we approve when he takes an escalated action, using violence that results in a bloody nose for the bully (Dupont & Clark, 1983) .

Now contrast Ralphie's actions in *A Christmas Story* with actions of siblings in a simple car ride. Brothers sit in the back seat, one smacks the other. The mother becomes angry and yells at the boy who delivered the blow. His excuse for striking his brother is, "He called me stupid." The mother will most likely not accept this reasoning noting that physical violence is never okay. So when this mother watched *A Christmas Story*, did she disapprove of Ralphie's actions against the bully? I would wager not. Watching the movie, we take on the perspective of the hero whose honor has been attacked; while driving the kids in the backseat of the car we are the Leviathan, the *deus ex machina*.

Parents and adults working with kids will often seek out and embrace a set of procedures to use with children and teens, a system or "program" to be used. The procedures in those programs are generally based on established valid principles (even though I disagree with many) and may be helpful to some children. There are an amazing number of programs purporting to help people working with children. I have personally been trained in dozens of programs with wide ranging premises from Freudian to Radical Behaviorism to Cognitive Theory and everything in between. The results of these programs in my personal story have always been mixed. Even though research from these programs is often positive, no one particular procedure or program is reported to universally "work." When we adults engage with a child or teen, we must ask ourselves, "Are we enemies defending our honor or are we the tentacle of the Leviathan maintaining order?" This distinction is often not discussed or understood by adults when a claim is made that a system, procedure, or approach did not "work." These programs are generally designed to change behaviors such as following adult instructions, interacting with peers in specific ways, or refraining from self-harm. A child's progress is measured by behaviors as this is what's observable and can be easily measured. Changing a child's behavior is often achievable with many different kinds of strategies, but the change necessary to satisfy an adult defending his or her honor is generally unachievable.

Many adults will demand "respect" from children and teens. When asked to explain what "respect" exactly entails, parents often offer a paradoxical concept, that children must follow adult instruction even if it's a non-preferred task. They must act like it's preferred, not hold any kind of animosity towards the parent, and be generally nice even if the parent is rude or obnoxious. All of this seems to point to the concept of "honor" — the underlying drive to overreact to any small insult in order to prevent future incidents.

The problem with honor fighting is that it quickly escalates. Homer recounts in *The Iliad* how the Trojan War was sparked when a Trojan noble named Paris took the wife of the King of Sparta. He didn't kidnap her, she came with him willingly, but the King was insulted. He called on his brother Agamemnon, King of Mycenae to aid him and the war was on (Homer & Lattimore, 1951). The middle ages is full of accounts of noble lords fighting long drawn out conflicts using conscripted troops because of some small insult at court, a drooping banner, the wrong kind of wine, etc. (Pinker, 2011). When both parties begin fighting for honor, someone can win, but the price can be high, remember the Montagues & Capulets or Hatfields & McCoys.

The feeling of being dishonored (disrespected) is always ready to bubble up, like a coiled snake or a loaded gun. It's an ancient component of our personal stories that is reaffirmed constantly. It's entrenched in our traditions, both at the level of families and entire cultural groups. When it comes to our own children, the tradition is even more powerful. Most cultures have beliefs regarding a child's "respect" of those older, especially family members. Fostering this sense of honor and respect is generally not a problem for most children, but at some point for some reason, the potential for an honor fight is always there. Children of immigrant families might struggle with this as the dominant western culture projects versions of "respect" that might contrast with their own. Of course, regional variations exist of the "normal" standard of respect as well. For example, southern and rural areas have been found to have higher incidences of "honor" based actions than urban centers (Pinker, 2011).

Fighting for honor is not inherently bad, it has served a purpose for the entire history of human civilization. It becomes problematic when it's not recognized and the escalation to be the victor is not a calculated decision but an emotional reaction, the coiled snake striking. I personally have fallen into this trap and felt a surge of animosity due to a child's actions, which prompted me to engage in a power struggle to not be "disrespected." Even when the child backed down, I always felt disappointed in myself because I let the need for honor drive my actions instead of what was best for the situation. Sometimes, I do feel the sense of being "disrespected" or "dishonored," but I have practiced to not let it dictate my behaviors. This can be extraordinarily difficult. It has always fascinated me that adults will expect teens to never engage in honor fighting, to stay cool when being verbally "attacked," but at the same time the adults don't have to live by the same expectations. For me, how can I expect a child to master a skill I haven't? To address this, adults can foster a sense of being the Leviathan.

The Leviathan is an authority above the conflict at hand. It may be biased and have its own agenda, but that agenda is based on calculated decisions and recognized moral values. Government policies are examples of this, such as the policy to "contain" communism in the second half of the twentieth century. This agenda brought the United States into several armed conflicts and many argue whether it was the best decision, but it was made based on a moral standard and a calculation of facts known at the time. It was not a knee-jerk reaction to prove strength and intimidate other nations.

When adults act as the Leviathan, we are enforcing the policies that were made prior to the emotional spike that accompanies being dishonored or disrespected. Taking this stance means accepting the role of the *deus ex machina*, the external solver of problems, who is not really part of the story. Imagine two teenage boys who have been slowly exchanging insults for several days. The attacks on each other's honor have escalated to squaring off physically but not yet to the point of violence. Insults are not only spouted from the two involved but also from their "friends" who surround and hurl taunts. It's a scene right out of Westside Story. A crowd of onlookers gather. The audience loves it, some kids shout "Fight!" More children come scrambling towards the group. A massive crowd now encircles the two boys. The onlookers all scream and shout for one to attack the other. Its high drama. Suddenly, a large adult bursts into the ring, he shouts forcefully to "Break apart," and communicates into a radio. The crowd surrounding disperses as more adults run to the group. One boy sensing the climax of the scene strikes with a punch. A melee ensues and the boy who attacked is restrained by security, while the victim is held back and escorted away.

In this typical schoolyard scene, the adults arrive like Athena or Zeus to resolve the situation based on established procedures. The adult will instruct the teens to end the standoff as he radios for backup. When one boy becomes physically dangerous, he is restrained (which has unique procedures of its own). At no point are the adults part of the narrative. They did not come to protect their own personal honor. The situation is intense and full of adrenaline, lots of problems can erupt. This is why adults in these positions are highly trained to take only actions dictated by policy and procedures, the same as a policeman or soldier. The need to stay cool and act from a position of calm authority can be critical in these emergency situations.

In actuality, all adults working with children and teens can develop this skill of being the Leviathan and take actions based on values and calculated decisions. The first step in achieving this is accepting the role and the Leviathan mindset. This means that after a conflict the story will not feel complete for either party as an honor wound may still exist and the teen remains angry and resentful. The teen does not feel in control. They feel robbed of creating an ending, so the story continues, which is just fine. Taking the role of Leviathan, the *deus ex machina*, is different than other roles we have discussed. It's outside the story and is the role required to appropriately manipulate a child's behaviors. Many professionals describe this as "setting limits."

Limit setting is not to be confused with fighting in honor duels with children by issuing escalating threats or punishments. When setting a limit from the Leviathan stance, it's often helpful to also validate the teen's story. For example, one might say, "I know Jim insulted you and you want to get even, but it's not okay to take revenge by hitting him." If the teen continues to march towards Jim to punch him in face, the next step is to remind him that he is in control of his actions but those actions trigger automatic responses and consequences. You can say, "I'm not going to try to stop you but if you keep walking towards Jim, I have to alert security and you'll have at least one day of detention." The adult can also provide alternatives to reach the same conclusion that the teen is searching for but is allowed by policy. "You can go make an appointment with the counselor to find a way to confront Jim appropriately for what he did." Let's say the teen turns back and yells profanity lined insults at the adult and then continues walking towards Jim. The adult might feel disrespected but they fall back on their training and simply call for security. All this sounds simple, but I have witnessed various versions of this scenario turn bad quickly. The adults in those cases allowed themselves to begin fighting for honor when their instructions were ignored. To be the Leviathan or *deus ex machina*, adults must make a conscious decision that no action from the teen will trigger an honor response. The adult must be clear about the policy and procedures they will base the limits on. If a child decides to take the path that the adult is against, the adult simply employs the previously decided actions, like calling the police if the teen is a danger to himself or others. Using force is sometimes necessary, but should only be done by those trained and authorized. When needed, parents can become part of this Leviathan, they can be the *deus ex machina* that sorts out the problem from superior authority, but no progress will be made from honor dueling.

15

IT'S ALL PART OF THE SHOW!

In the film *The Rocketeer,* a 30's era racing pilot named Cliff Secord finds a jetpack stashed in his hangar. It's a prototype developed by Howard Hughes and Cliff's not sure what to do with it at first. Perhaps it's a way to make some money since he's part of a flying circus, a show featuring aviation stunts. As he practices using the device, he keeps it a secret, rightly deducing that several people are looking for the device. Cliff's hand is forced one day when an old friend decides to cover for him after he runs late for a show. This friend is a WWI pilot, but hasn't flown in years. Cliff's old friend takes flight in the jalopy plane that Cliff was to fly and almost immediately something goes wrong. As the action hero of the film, Cliff must do something to help. He straps on the jetpack, dons a finned art deco style helmet, and blasts off to save the plane that's in obvious peril. As the audience looks on aghast at what they see, the owner of the show is told by a flunky to evacuate the crowd, but the boss is concerned about giving all these people a refund and losing money. His solution is to announce, "It's all part of the show!" As the flying jetpack hero rescues the injured pilot, the evacuated plane crashes into a truck, and the Rocketeer flies off into the distance. The audience is told repeatedly, "It's all part of the show." They cheer in approval (Gordon, Gordon, Levon & Johnston, 1991).

This idea of pretending to make an error is a trope that pervades many types of entertainment. We as audiences are often fooled by this tactic. Magicians, clowns, circus acrobats, all have used this trick to make a show more interesting. To pretend that something is wrong to invoke a sense of fear and then show how it was actually all planned provides the audience with a sense of wonder and amazement. The flip of using it to cover when an unforeseen problem arises is also a handy tactic. Audiences are already trained to accept the purposeful error explanation.

When dealing with children, we may use both strategies. Principal Skinner in *The Simpsons* once remarked to a teacher, "We both know these kids have no future!" Then, realizing he was in the middle of the cafeteria, surrounded by children, stood straight and declared in a loving tone, "Prove me wrong kids, prove me wrong." (Crittenden & Scott III, 1995). Most adults will readily admit they're not perfect, but a strange kind of expectation can be found in the stories parents create for themselves. They may inherently envision themselves as Gregory Peck's character Atticus from *To Kill a Mockingbird*. Atticus is a strong stoic adult who will do what is right and pass these values down to the children (Pakula & Mulligan, 1962). However, many actually feel more like Steve Martin in *Parenthood*, just trying to figure things out on a daily basis, full of anxiety and dread (Grazer & Howard, 1989). We all love the Steve Martin character, but his is not the story we want to tell. This sets up a conflict with an internal drive to be Gregory Peck versus a daily life experience of feeling like Steve Martin.

Parents may find all kinds of ways to pretend they are the wise all-knowing captain of the ship, to spin their actions into something that makes sense in the story they want to tell, to be the hero they want to be. Parents may also realize they are not playing the ideal part and search desperately to transform themselves into that character. Many have often looked to me for a way to be this type of person, they want to know how to "do it right." They point to friends and family who seem to be parenting with "better" results than they're achieving. What is not fully appreciated in these analyses is the degree to which the ideal parents are faking it, claiming "It's all part of the show."

As we have examined throughout this book, feeling like an effective parent comes down to feeling in control of the story being played out. Knowing that it's the way it "should" be. We want to ensure kids and teens are fighting the villains we want them to fight, having a love interest we approve of, and choosing a mentor that matches our values. This ideal and perfect story is what we attempt to create by our behaviors, which are not necessarily conscious choices.

A common belief amongst new parents is that a special method exists to create this ideal child. They might say, "I won't make the mistakes my parents did." They embrace a parenting "system" that gives step by step directions for raising the perfect kid. Often these systems are based around the idea of conditioning a child, to use external stimulus to guide and shape behaviors. Contrastingly, a system might focus on how to effectively communicate with kids and work towards mutual compromises. Many of these programs are quite valuable and effective, but in specific ways. Parents will use a system diligently and often believe that it "works," but just not all the time. So, they may then search for a new better system because they believe the perfect method is out there to create the ideal kid. Of course, most parents will say they don't need a child to be "perfect," but they do want a child who matches their expectations most of the time. Unfortunately, this "perfect" system to create the ideal child does not exist. Again, most parents know this, but do they genuinely "believe" it?

The problem is that systems, methods and programs generally assume that life is a series of cause and effect chains, like billiard balls hitting into each other. This conceptualization is inherently flawed because our stories are always in motion and interacting in countless intricate ways. When working with children and using any type of intervention, the key to getting it to "work" is realizing that the story never stops. All people (and organisms) create behaviors to bring the story back into alignment, back to what is expected and desired. Behaviors are not a cause and effect chain, they are a byproduct and method of maintaining this control (Carey, 2006). Imagine driving down a road, the lane twists to the left, the driver turns the wheel to the left to keep between the lanes' stripes. If the stripes on the road twist to the right, the driver turns to the right keeping inside the lines. There is no cause and effect, the road twists did not cause the wheel turning. The behaviors are an observable method of an organism trying to control their perception of what's important. When working with children, it can be conceptualized as if they are walking down a road with large ditches on either side. They begin to veer to the right, we call out, "Move to the left." Later, they begin to veer too far to the left and we call out, "Move to the right." These are opposite instructions yet both are appropriate and needed to guide the child on the path we see and they do not. Depending on what's happening, we might give a small call to warn them, we might point out something interesting in the middle of the road, or we might throw a rock to startle them towards the middle. Many methods and strategies can be used to guide the progress but the walking never ends. A gentle call might be enough at one point but the rock at another. However, what happens when we reach a fork in the road?

In our stories (and screenplays), there is a moment generally called "the point of no return" which is the moment that the character commits himself to the mission and goal (McKee, 1997). He might have been dabbling before but now the stakes have raised and the goal must be attained. This requires accepting the risks and limitations of the story. The consequences of this point are like choosing a fork in the road. Once a direction is chosen, the other path is lost forever. When the Rocketeer made the choice to rescue his friend, he let the secret out and began being pursued by villains. He made a moral and value driven decision to act as he felt a hero should, but now the rest of the story involves running from gangsters, Nazis, and the FBI. Every decision a character makes to move in one direction means the other direction is closed off. In economics, this is known as "opportunity cost." When I choose to buy something, I must give up all the things I could have bought instead. A common trope that illustrates this point is when the superhero must give up his relationship to continue his crusade. Superman tries to have a relationship with Lois Lane in the second *Superman* film, but he is forced to give up his powers. After this happens, he realizes that he can't let the villains win and reverses his decision, giving up the relationship to gain his powers back (Spengler & Lester, 1980). Throughout the incarnations of Batman, he often must play the part of the buffoon in public as Bruce Wayne. He gives up having relationships and public respect in order to continue his crusade against crime (Weldon, 2017). This element of our stories is difficult for many adults to accept when working with kids.

If I choose to use threats and bribes to manipulate a child's choices, then in his story I have become a bank, a business, something that uses legalistic rules to dole out or take away desired resources. This means I am not the friend who provides warm validation, shares secrets, and is fun to hang out with. Of course, these roles might shift back and forth, but then they are affected, colored, and flavored by the previous relationship. Flipping back and forth frequently will have an effect on the story, just as staying true to one role has an effect. Neither is necessarily "good" or "bad." The point is accepting that both roles cannot be held at the same time and taking on one role means shifting the story as it cascades through time.

I have often heard adults claim that a system of intervention didn't work. For example, a boy is upset at being told he cannot participate in some activity, maybe playing video games. The adult is taking a behavioral stance, the role of police or enforcer. The child is ordered to go to his room or he will lose video game time tomorrow. So, he then screams a profanity and makes statements like, "I hate you!" He then jumps to his feet, dashes to his room and slams the door. The parents make the case that the threat of losing video games didn't work. But, to me it certainly did work because the goal of the intervention was for the child to go to his room, which was accomplished. Parents says it didn't work because of the rude way the child went to his room. However, by taking on the role of the villain and police enforcer of rules, we accept that other roles are not being chosen. In these scenarios, adults will often go to the child at some point not too long after the encounter and attempt to be the soothing friend and mentor. They make the case that what happened before was "All part of the show" and was a necessary part of being a parent. Sure, that's a good argument, but the child isn't likely to hear this message because he is still locked in the previous role. He might yell and scream provoking the adult to resume the enforcer role and issue more punishments. Alternatively, the child nods and agrees in compliant understanding, but this has the flavor of submitting to authority, of agreeing with the boss just to stay out of trouble. Adults often like to have "heart to heart" talks with teens just after issuing punishments. The teen nods in agreement and the adult feels like real "progress" was made. Was it really or was the teen just telling the adult what they wanted to hear? Because the punishments were issued, the later conversation is tainted. This is not to say to avoid using punishments, but it's to warn that use of threats, angry tones, shame, guilt, and sarcasm all come with a downside. They may be great at changing a behavior, but the effect on the story and roles each person takes are best acknowledged. Knowing that this choice is being made can help adults decide if it is really necessary.

Many kids will stop in their tracks if an adult shouts in an angry tone. This is an automatic response to "danger." Shouting gets quick and immediate results. However, I have now changed the story, the roles, and the relationship. The child will react in some way to this in the future. I have seen adults shout at kids in mean tones and the child feels immense guilt and shame, which prompts them to get quiet and follow the adult's directions. Moments later, the adult says, "Why are you always sad all the time?" I have personally endeavored to use my "angry tone" as a weapon of last resort, something that I have in reserve if needed for immediate responses. However, I have to accept that after using it the child or teen will be annoyed and our relationship has changed. On many occasions, especially when potential physical danger is involved, I've decided that the cost was worth the benefit. When adults shout in angry tones constantly, they will diminish the effectiveness of the intervention and they will continue to create an adversarial relationship. That is a choice I think most parents would avoid.

Many may accept these ideas, but there is generally a nagging feeling that there must be a way to guide children in their story and push them in ways that will make them a success with 99% certain results. In the sci-fi film *Soldier*, a program in the distant future selects children from birth based on temperament. Over their lives, the government conditions these children to be stoic warriors who follow orders, ignore pain, and will respond with brutal violence but no emotional connection (Weintraub & Anderson, 1998). To me, this is similar to guiding a child's story in specific directions towards concrete goals all the time. Many Olympic athletes will report beginning their sport at ages earlier than 3 and their skill was fostered and pushed by adults to be the peak of performance, but there were costs as well. We've all seen the "pageant" mother or the "sports" father who pushes his or her child towards a certain skill perfection. This may achieve the specific desired results but at the cost of relationships. In *Soldier*, the super conditioned warriors work well until new genetically engineered versions take their place. Kurt Russell plays a soldier who is stranded with "normal" people, but he cannot fit in. He reacts in strange and unpredictably violent ways and he's cold and unemotional.

On the flip side, we have parents who attempt to foster skills like independence, critical thinking, and problem solving. Many professional educators codify these goals into a school's official objectives. However, what does this really mean? A school full of Ferris Buellers can identify the absurdity of the education system, identify the flaws, and take advantage of them (Jacobson & Hughes, 1986). Many of my students who were expelled from public school matched this description. They could find a way out of any situation, point out loopholes in whatever behavior contract that was proposed, and infuriate adults with their debate skills. This was not what most adults had in mind when they created their initial goals of critical thinking.

In the film *V for Vendetta*, based on the comic book by Alan Moore, the main character Evey is seemingly captured by the fascist government secret police. She is held in a dingy, disgusting cell. Her head is shaved and she is fed gruel. In this state, the officials interrogate her with many types of torture attempting to get information about an anarchistic freedom fighter named "V." Evey doesn't have any information, but she is still tortured repeatedly. She finds solace in a story that was handwritten on a scroll of toilet paper and hidden in a crack of the wall, seemingly passed from the cell next door. The story on this roll relates how another young woman was taken prisoner and also tortured. Evey finds strength in knowing she is not alone and decides to accept her fate and not give into the cruel authorities. In the end, an official comes to her door and informs her that her execution order has been issued unless she cooperates. Evey calmly informs the man that she is now prepared to die for her convictions. The door is left open, the guard is then gone. Evey is confused and makes her way down the hall. It is filled with mannequins in military uniforms, the walls are faux rock. She enters another room to realize that she was never a prisoner, "It was all part of the show." V had tricked her. He was the one putting her through the torture and he planted the story in the crack of the wall. When asked why, V describes his plan to help Evey find inner strength, to be forced to decide what she most values. He believed this is what is required to win the day in the future. Evey is stunned and heartbroken but she understands. She is grateful and yet knows their relationship will never be the same and she must leave (Moore, & Lloyd, 1990).

Several stories and movies have illustrated this approach to conditioning a person. Shaping their story by taking on a role that will result in the ending that we desire. When we seek a way to create a "good" child, it's helpful to remember these choices. Are these choices made intentionally or accidentally? V made the choice to put Evey though a horrible situation because he believed the lesson was worth the pain and suffering that she went through. Most would argue that this went too far, that tortuous abuse is never an acceptable method to push another person in a certain direction. Even if not abused as Evey was, children and teens still feel the anguish and pain when adults act as V did to create scenarios of great hardship to teach a lesson.

In some cases, parents are forced to make a hard choice and send children to "wilderness boot camp" or residential treatment centers where the rules are strictly enforced every minute of the day and freedom is earned in small increments over long periods of time. These choices are made because circumstances forced a drastic intervention into the story. The parent decided that the damage to the relationship was worth it to save the child from the direction their story was taking, perhaps due to drug addiction, criminal activity, or severe mental illness.

Parents who are forced to make these choices often feel that they did something wrong, while other parents feel that they can avoid these circumstances with specific methods of parenting. The reality is that each child's story is unique to that child and storylines of all types are twisting and turning constantly. There are no interventions that will guarantee "success." Young men and women who are incarcerated may say, "I wish my parents were more strict. They let me get away with anything and now I'm here." So, parents decide that they need to be strict. Then another inmate states, "If my parents would have just given me some space. They controlled everything, I couldn't take it, drugs were my only way out." So, the conclusion is to give teens more space. How about the young offender who says, "My parents are middle class drones, they don't get it. I don't care what society says, I'll do whatever drug I want." So parents must...?

The truth is that when we look back to make sense of our story, the plot has to make sense, a villain must be created, blame must be placed, and a theme must emerge. Asking billionaires why they are so successful is pointless because they don't know why they are successful, they only know the story they tell themselves. This is fine if you want to hear a good story, but it's not helpful for making life strategies. In the end, it boils down to making deliberate decisions by asking ourselves these questions: What is important? What do I value? What specific goals do I have for my kids? What am I willing to sacrifice for these goals? As situations arise, we make decisions and take on roles that push the child's story in the direction we have decided we want it to go. This is what "good" parenting entails. The results will always be mixed, will always have drama, and will always be epic. That's why it's great!

REFERENCES

American Psychiatric Association. (2013). *Diagnostic and statistical manual of mental disorders: DSM-5.* Washington, D.C: American Psychiatric Association.

Ariely, D. (2010). *Predictably irrational: The hidden forces that shape our decisions.* New York, NY: Harper Perennial.

Bashford, A. & Levine, P.(2012). *The Oxford handbook of the history of eugenics.* Oxford: Oxford University Press.

Bell, R.G., Linson, A. & Fincher, D. (1999). *Fight Club.* United States: Twentieth Century Fox Film Corporation.

Bernhard, H. & Donner, R. (1985). *The Goonies.* United States: Warner Bros.

Bevan, T., Fellner, E., Park, N., & Wright, E. (2007). *Hot Fuzz.* United Kingdom: Universal Pictures.

Bombyk, D., Feldman, E.S., & Dante, J. (1985). *Explorers.* United States: Paramount Pictures.

Boorman, J. (1981). *Excalibur.* United States: Orion Pictures.

Broccoli, A., Saltzman, H. & Hamilton, G. (1964). *Goldfinger.* United Kingdom: United Artist.

Brooks, D. (2012). *The social animal: The hidden sources of love.* New York, NY: Random House Trade Paperbacks.

Campbell, J. (1949). *Hero with a thousand faces.* Princeton, NJ : Princeton University Press.

Canton N., Gale, B. & Zemeckis, R. (1985). *Back to the Future*. Universal Pictures.

Cartwright, M. (2012, July 09). Hercules. *Ancient History Encyclopedia.* Retrieved from http://www.ancient.eu/hercules/

Carey, T. A. (2006). *The method of levels: How to do psychotherapy without getting in the way.* Hayward, CA: Living Control Systems Pub.

Chartoff, R., Winkler, I. & Avildsen, J. (1976). *Rocky*. United States: United Artists.

Crittenden, J. & Scott III, S. (16 April 1995) "The PTA Disbands." *The Simpsons.* United States: 20th Century Fox Television.

Damasio, A. R. (2010). *Self comes to mind: Constructing the conscious brain.* New York, NY: Pantheon Books.

Davis, P., Panzer, W. & Mulcahy R. (1986). *Highlander.* United Kingdom: Twentieth Century Fox Film Corporation.

De Laurentiis, R., Pressman, E. & Fleischer, R. (1984). *Conan the Destroyer.* United States: Universal Pictures.

Diamond, J. M. (1997). *Guns, germs, and steel: The fates of human societies.* New York, NY: W.W. Norton & Co.

Disney, W & Reitherman, W. (1963). *The Sword in the Stone.* United States: Buena Vista Pictures.

Donner, L.S., Winter, R., & Singer, B. (2000). *X-men*. United States: Twentieth Century Fox Film Corporation.

Duclon, D. & Dielhenn, A. (19 Jan. 1986) "Cherie Lifesaver." Duclon, D. *Punky Brewster.* United States: National Broadcasting Company.

Dumas, A., Maquet, A., & Fiorentino, P. A. (1934). *The count of monte cristo.* London: J.M. Dent & Sons.

Dunning, B. "Who Were the Berserkers?" *Skeptoid Podcast.* Skeptoid Media, 7 Feb 2017.Web. 18 May 2017. <http://skeptoid.com/episodes/4557>

Dupont, R. & Clark, B. (1983). *A Christmas Story.* United States: Metro Goldwyn-Mayer.

Feitshans, B., Shusett, R., & Verhoeven, P. (1990). *Total Recall.* United States: Tristar Pictures.

Garland, R., & Teaching Company. (2015). *The other side of history: Daily life in the ancient world.* Chantilly, Va.: Teaching Company.

Gatto, J. T. (2001). *The underground history of American education: A schoolteacher's intimate investigation into the problem of modern schooling.* New York, NY: Oxford Village Press

Gordon, C., Gordon L., Levon, L., & Johnston, J. (1991). *The Rocketeer.* United States: Buena Vista Pictures.

Gould, S.J. (1994). "Curveball." *The New Yorker,* 28 Nov. 1994.

Grazer, B. & Howard, R. (1989). *Parenthood.* United States: Universal Pictures.

Hanks, T., Rapke, J., Starkey, S., & Zemeckis, R. (2000). *Cast Away.* United States: Twentieth Century Fox Film Corporation.

Hanley, T. (2014). *Wonder woman unbound: The curious history of the world's most famous heroine.* Chicago: Chicago Review Press.

Hart, J., Coppola, F. F. & Branagh, K. (1994). *Mary Shelley's Frankenstein*. United States: Tristar Pictures.

Herbert, F. (1965). *Dune*. New York, NY: Chilton Books.

Herbert, F. (1981). *God emperor of dune*. New York, NY: Berkley.

Herrnstein, R. J., & Murray, C. A. (1996). *The bell curve: Intelligence and class structure in American life*. New York, NY: Simon & Schuster.

Heyman, D. & Columbus, C. (2001). *Harry Potter and the Sorcerer's Stone*. United Kingdom: Warner Bros.

Hiatt, B. (2014, May 26). The True Origins of the X-men. *Rolling Stone*, Retrieved from http://www.rollingstone.com/movies/news/the true-origins-of-x-men-2014052

Hill, W., Giler, D., Carroll, G. & Scott, R. (1979). *Alien*. United Kingdom: Twentieth Century Fox Film Corporation.

Hobbes, T., & Macpherson, C. B. (2003). *Leviathan*. London: Penguin.

Homer, & Lattimore, R. (1951). *The iliad*. Chicago, IL: University of Chicago Press.

Homer, & Fitzgerald, R. (1990). *The odyssey*. New York, NY: Vintage Books.

Jacobson, T. & Hughes, J. (1986). *Ferris Bueller's Day Off*. United States: Paramount Pictures.

Kahneman, D. (2015). *Thinking, fast and slow*. New York, NY: Farrar, Straus and Giroux.

Kaminski, M. (2008). *The secret history of star wars: The art of storytelling and the making of a modern epic.* Kingston, Ont: Legacy Books Press.

Kazanjian, H. & Marquand, R. (1983). *Star Wars: Episode VI - Return of the Jedi.* United States: Twentieth Century Fox Film Corporation.

Kurtz, G. & Kershner, I. (1980). *The Empire Strikes Back.* United States: Twentieth Century-Fox Film Corporation.

Kurtz, G. & Lucas, G. (1977). *Star Wars: Episode IV - A New Hope.* United States: Twentieth Century Fox Film Corporation.

Laemmle C. & Whale, J. (1931). *Frankenstein.* United States: Universal Pictures.

Levinson, M. & Daniel, R. (1985). *Teen Wolf.* United States: Atlantic Releasing Corporation.

Lindelof, D. & Abrams, J. J. (2009). *Star Trek.* United States: Paramount Pictures.

Malory, T., & Rhys, J. (1906). *Le morte d'Arthur*: Printed by William Caxton, 1485. London: Dent.

Mancuso, F. & Frankenheimer, J. (1998). *Ronin.* United States: United Artist.

Mark, J. J. (2010, October 13). Gilgamesh. *Ancient History Encyclopedia.* Retrieved from http://www.ancient.eu/gilgamesh/

Marshall, F. & Spielberg, S. (1981). *Raiders of the Lost Ark.* United States: Paramount Pictures.

McKee, R. (1997). *Story: Substance, structure, style.* New York, NY: ReganBooks.

Michelinie, D. (1996). Hazard's Choice. *Superman in Action Comics*, 1(719).

Miller, F., Janson, K., Varley, L., Costanza, J., & Klein, T. (2015). *Batman, the dark knight saga deluxe edition.* Burbank, CA: DC Comics.

Mlodinow, L. (2009). *The drunkard's walk: How randomness rules our lives.* New York, NY: Pantheon Books.

Moore, A., & Lloyd, D. (1990). *V is for vendetta.* London: Titan.

Moore, A. (1986). *Watchmen.* New York, NY: DC Comics.

Novella, S., Novella, S., & Teaching Company. (2015). *Your deceptive mind: A scientific guide to critical thinking skills.* Chantilly, Va: Teaching Co.

Novella, S., & Teaching Company. (2010). *Medical myths, lies, and half-truths: What we think we know may be hurting us.* Chantilly, VA: Teaching Co.

Pakula, A. & Mulligan, R. (1962). *To Kill a Mockingbird.* United States: Universal Pictures.

Pinker, S. (2011). *The better angels of our nature: Why violence has declined.* New York, NY: Viking.

"PTSD: National Center for PTSD." *U.S. Department of Veterans Affairs*, 18 May 2017, https://www.ptsd.va.gov/public/treatment/therapy-med/treatment-ptsd.asp.

Reitman, I. (1984). *Ghostbusters.* United States: Columbia Pictures.

Reitman, I. (1989). *Ghostbusters II.* United States: Columbia Pictures.

Roberson, C., Denton, S. E., Castro, R., & Evely, B. (2015). *Doc Savage: Volume 1*. Mt. Laurel, NJ: Dynamite Entertainment,

Rosenthal, R., & Jacobson, L. (1968). *Pygmalion in the classroom: Teacher expectation and pupils' intellectual development*. New York, NY: Holt, Rinehart and Winston.

Rowling, J. K. (1997). *Harry potter and the sorcerer's stone* (1). New York, NY: Scholastic Press.

Scheinman, A. & Reiner, R. (1987). *The Princess Bride*. United States: Twentieth Century Fox Film Corporation.

Selvin, Steve (1975). A problem in probability (letter to the editor). *American Statistician,* 29 (1), 67.

Shelley, M. W., & Rieger, J. (1982). Frankenstein, or, The modern Prometheus, the 1818 text. Chicago: University of Chicago Press.

Shippey, T., & Teaching Company. (2015). *Heroes and legends: The most influential characters of literature*. Chantilly, Va: Teaching Co.

Siegel, D. J. (2011). *Mindsight: The new science of personal transformation*. New York, NY: Bantam Books Trade Paperbacks.

Siegel, D. (1971). *Dirty Harry*. United States: Warner Bros.

Silver, J., Wachowski, L. & Wachowski L. (1999). *The Matrix*. United States: Warner Bros.

Silver, J., Gordon, L. & McTiernan, J. (1988). *Die Hard*. United States: Twentieth Century Fox Film Corporation.

Smith, E. E. (1950). *Galactic patrol*. New York, NY: Pyramid Books.

Spengler, P. & Lester, R. (1980). *Superman II*. United States: Warner Bros.

Tapert, R. & Raimi, S. (1987). *Evil Dead II*. United States: Rosebud Releasing Corporation.

Tapert, R. & Raimi, S. (1992). *Army of Darkness*. United States: Universal Pictures.

Tolkien, J. R. R. (1954, 1999). *The fellowship of the ring*. New York, NY: HarperCollins.

Tye, L. (2013). *Superman: The high-flying history of America's most enduring hero*. New York, NY: Random House.

Waid, M. (2001). *JLA: Tower of babel*. New York, NY: DC Comics.

Watts, A. (1966). *The book: On the taboo against knowing who you are*. New York, NY: Pantheon Books.

Watts, A. (1957). *The way of zen*. New York, NY: Vintage Books.

Watts, R. & Spielberg, S. (1989). *Indiana Jones and the Last Crusade*. United State: Paramount Pictures.

Watts, R. & Spielberg, S. (1984). *Indiana Jones and the Temple of Doom*. United States: Paramount Pictures.

Weldon, G. (2017). *The caped crusade: Batman and the rise of nerd culture*. New York, NY: Simon & Schuster.

Weintraub, J. & Anderson, P. (1998). *Soldier*. United Kingdom: Warner Bros.

Whitbrook, J. (2015, March 25). A Brief History of Daredevil, Marvel's Latest TV Hero. *Gizmodo*, Retrieved from http://io9.gizmodo.com/a-brief-history-of-daredevil-marvels-latest-tv-hero-1693644683

White, M. (2007). *Maps of narrative practice*. New York, NY: W W Norton & Co.

White, T. H. (1987). *The once and future king*. New York, NY: Ace Books.

Williams, O. (2016, April 29). *The Punisher: A Complete History. Empire*, Retrieved from http://www.empireonline.com/movies/features/punisher-complete-history/

Vogler, C. (1998). *The writer's journey: Mythic structure for writers*. Studio City, CA: M. Wiese Productions.

ABOUT THE AUTHOR

Dr. Kyle Erwin has worked for over 15 years as a public school teacher, special education teacher, school administrator, and psychotherapist. In these positions, he has worked primarily with teens and families to address difficulties related to autism spectrum disorder, oppositional defiant disorder, obsessive compulsive disorder, depression, and attention deficit/hyperactivity disorder.

Dr. Erwin has also worked extensively to aid children and parents with school based issues related to social emotional struggles. He has also aided teachers and psychotherapists to improve school programs in order to best meet the individual needs of adolescents.

He holds a bachelor's degree in History Education from Northern Arizona University, master's and doctorate degrees in Education from the University of Southern California, and a master's in Marital and Family Therapy from Alliant International University.

www.ingramcontent.com/pod-product-compliance
Lightning Source LLC
LaVergne TN
LVHW051600070426
835507LV00021B/2673